Where's IT Going?

Prospects for Tomorrow

Where's IT Going?

Ian Pearson & Chris Winter

Thames & Hudson

First published in the United Kingdom in 2000 by Thames & Hudson Ltd,
181A High Holborn, London WCIV 7QX

British Library Cataloguing-in-Publication Data
A catalogue record for this book is available from the British Library

ISBN 0-500-28137-8

Printed and bound in Slovenia by Mladinska Knjiga

CONTENTS

PREFACE

Visit any large company and ask to look round its IT department. You can be sure that it will exist, and equally sure that you will be shown computers and network hardware. The company may be proud of its IT department, or it may moan about its lack of impact on the business. It does not really matter, either view is the same: IT is to do with *technology*, a special part of the company bolted on to the exterior of how it works – controlled, managed and worried over for its expense. This book is about something very different. When IT is separate and special we have not understood it at all, let alone used or seen its full potential. We will show how a few simple technological developments will lead to IT being an integral part of everyone's daily life.

The ability to communicate is a profound and key part of functioning as a social being. When humankind could only shout, its communities were small tribal entities. Writing and the city-state came into being at around the same time. This is no surprise, for the abilities to transmit information reliably over distance and to store it are both essential to a wider government. Improving road and sea communications increased the capacity of such messages, until finally the telegraph was invented, and then the telephone. These inventions became key components of industrialized societies, coordinating companies that were spread across nations. The worldwide web and the Internet are now initiating further changes, as people around the globe can organize their actions ever more effectively, allowing minorities to find supporters, and individuals to take on conglomerates.

The real importance of the IT revolution is that it enables many new forms of communication, and thus new forms of social and corporate organization. Everything that changes the way we communicate will change society.

Even more interesting, in the near future, machines talking to machines will overtake people as the main consumers of communication capacity. These machines will soon form organizations and behaviour patterns that will be difficult for us to predict. An example of this is the emergence of 'information waves' that can overwhelm financial trading systems as machines trade automatically.

The two great driving forces in IT are normally seen to be the growth in transmission capacity (bandwidth), brought about through developments in optical systems, radio technology and satellites, and the increase in computing power. Both are seen as bringing the cost of IT down, and thus as increasing accessibility. However, these are merely the basic instruments that will be used to shape the real revolution in information technology.

There are many harbingers of a much richer IT world. There will be intelligent agents that work for you; the computer will become an invisible part of your environment as chips in every device communicate with each other; the interface will understand your speech, attune to your mood, be intuitive to use, and even respond to your emotions; smart materials will adapt to the changing worlds; and nano-robots will swarm into every crevice. The whole environment will seek to serve you and to shape itself to you wherever you go. Beyond that lie computers that will evolve their own programs and hardware; that will help you create artistic masterpieces of your own; and that will bring books, music and films to life. These living computers will be one step from life itself. Artificial life, one of the most recent disciplines in computer science, will be the major force of the twenty-first century. It will bring us challenges and opportunities that are difficult to comprehend.

To try to capture the essence of all these changes, we have arranged the book into three sections. The first deals with the major technologies of the future, many of which will make 1990s computers look very strange as they change the nature of computing completely. The second section looks at the impact of these technologies on certain areas of society, selected because we feel they are discussed less elsewhere and are quite often new. A full picture of our views on how IT will change society would otherwise take up many more pages than we have here. The final section is an attempt to suggest what lies slightly further ahead in the future, and the problems and challenges of how we deal with machines that appear smarter than us.

Many books have been written about single aspects of the IT revolution, or have listed interesting possibilities. Readers are advised to look at as many as possible, because it is the wider picture that is important, not the fine detail. The broad brushstrokes will be correct; the detail, probably wrong. Such is the nature of predicting the future. The aim of this book is twofold: firstly, to bring a range of possibilities to the fore that have not been previously explored; and secondly, to show that IT is not something special and separate. It will be wrapped into everything we do. In the future IT is it.

PART I

TECHNOLOGY

For many people, the future of IT is based around the idea that bandwidth – the capacity to move information around – and computing – the power to process information – will simply go on increasing, so that eventually we will have an excess of both. At that point information will be free.

This is a wonderful, if somewhat naïve, view of the future, and it hardly begins to highlight the really important issues. It is like judging car development by saying that all that matters is that they can go faster or use less petrol. If you want to know about whether ATM or WDM is the best technology for optical communications, or whether DECT will displace GSM, then you are reading the wrong book. These are questions of detail, with little significance in the broader picture of what the future of IT is.

The questions that really matter are more along the lines of: Is computing just going to get faster, or will it change in character? Will computers be easier to use? Where will I find computers – in the home, the office, or on my arm?

This section tries to cover these new technology issues and their impact on the basic direction of IT. Some of its conclusions are challenging: programming will move out of the hands of programmers; analogue computing will make a comeback; and computers will become inconspicuous or even invisible. However, to predict the future you must analyse not only the trends but also the points of major change.

I

COMMUNICATIONS

Network Control and ANTS
Computers were first built as stand-alone machines; only much later was networking 'bolted on' to the basic machine architecture. Similarly, telephony was originally designed for individuals to talk to one another on a one-to-one basis; only later came the ideas of multiple parties (conference calls) and data or machine networks overlaid on the voice circuits. In addition, the need to 'manage', that is to control, the entire network from the centre runs deep in the souls of telecommunication providers.

Thus, neither machine nor network have ever really been built from the ground up for highly distributed autonomous operation. In contrast, most biological organisms display a number of properties that are immensely desirable in networks, such as autonomy, multi-variable load balancing, robustness to component damage, self-healing, etc. One of the great trends for the future will be the development of these and other lifelike properties into computers and networks. Much of this book touches on the rise and impact of such a living machine.

In the earliest days of telephony, a connection between two tele-phones was made through a 'circuit' – an end-to-end wire dedicated exclusively to a single pair of users. The 'intelligence' in the network arose from the way that human operators handled and routed the calls to their correct destination. Initially, these operators were the very messenger boys who had been made redundant by the new service, although women, who were found to be more reliable, soon replaced them. Eventually, however, automatic switches supplanted the manual operators altogether. A side-effect of this automation was that the network became less intelligent, albeit much cheaper to run.

Since those early days, telecommunications companies have been striving constantly to make the network intelligent once again. Modern data networks break the information down into 'packets', each of which contains enough information to find its own way around the network. Examples of such networks include those using TCP-IP (the backbone of the Internet) and the telephony equivalent ATM (asynchronous transfer mode). However, these networks are still surprisingly dumb, with the packets containing little more than the address of the place they are trying to get to and a simple data segment. A great deal of effort, therefore, still goes into trying to put the human intelligence back into the switches.

The attempt to make the telephone switches more intelligent has led to the creation of the biggest computer programs ever written, containing up to a hundred million lines of code, and created by thousands of programmers. These programs are still only a pale imitation of the original human operators, however. A simple way to imagine the future would be to assume that such programs will just continue to be made larger. But another, radical approach has also been proposed: to mimic biology.

One of the ideas to emerge from this area of work is that of Autonomous Network Telephers – or ANTs – inspired by their biological namesakes. Imagine that every packet in the network contained a small piece of code telling the switch what it wanted to do, essentially a 'smart' packet. Instead of being like water piped round the network, the packets become like ants, scurrying around in a semi-intelligent manner and collectively performing as a single efficient organism. Ant colonies operate without a large central intelligence; they consist of many small, cooperating entities that perform complex tasks in a productive and robust manner. This is the analogy now being used to design the next generation of networks. Rather than making large programs, the new approach is to make every packet a little bit intelligent, like an ant, and then have millions of simple entities that interact with each other.

At appropriate processors, an ANT could unpack its code for execution by the processor. This code could contain various types of information, such as: code that is executed in the network; code that is executed at the destination; routing requests; processing instructions; information about following ANTs; addresses (home or destination); or route information. ANTs could thus be used for network signalling, network management, fault location and repair, software updates, and many other network functions, as well as user-oriented functions. The essential difference between an ANT and an ATM cell is that an ANT can pass instructions to processors regarding its own function and control. It is effectively an intelligent cell.

These antlike programs have a similarity to computer viruses: they scamper round the network, interact with each other and run the operation. They can be made adaptive so that each packet learns how to work with others and how to perform its task better. Just as a single human brain cell is not particularly powerful in itself, each individual ANT has very little intelligence, but the combined effect is profound, bringing intelligence and life to the network.

Eventually, such lifelike networks will take over. The current 'dumb' ones are simply too complex for us to continue building them ever larger. There will be a whole raft of changes that come with the change in network structure. The complicated tariff system loosely based on distance, bandwidth and utility will be replaced by simpler mechanisms. The traditional control mentality of the telecommunications companies will have to change to accept autonomy and intelligence in the network. The equally complicated regulatory environment will break down, since such autonomous networks will act in ways that circumvent and confuse regulations; and managerial systems will have to be simplified as well.

The range of possible services using intelligent packets is immense, particularly when they can recombine, breed, wait for partners, act collectively, etc. Furthermore, ANTs are programmed by looking for natural analogies or by evolving the appropriate behaviour. Biology has had a 500-million-year head start in learning how to make complex systems stable and self-organizing. This approach avoids engineers' having to learn how to build large central systems because it allows them to build small, decentralized ones.

The future of networks is that they will appear to be alive and intelligent to the user. The engineers who build them will have to learn a whole new way of thinking, less based on instruction, command and control, and more based on influencing, teaching and persuading. Perhaps they will find more inspiration from schoolteachers and biologists than from textbooks on programming.

II

COMPUTING

Computing Techniques

Today we build an electronic digital computer and program it with a set of simple logical instructions. We suppress all noise (an electrical term meaning random imperfections – all systems have some noise) and uncertainty, and remain in complete control (in theory) of what happens to every bit of information in the system. In doing so, we trap ourselves in a set of very difficult problems. How do you gently fade memory away as it is no longer needed? Everything is preserved perfectly or not at all. How can the system learn if you have control over all its states? Today's computers can learn only what they already nearly know. All the smart stuff comes out of the programmer's head in the way he or she built the system. This is hardly the way to build a computer that can do things that we cannot.

Quantum, optical, chemical, analogue and evolutionary computers all offer opportunities to rethink completely the way we do computing. Unfortunately, these machines often try to mimic electronic digital computers rather than exploit their own advantages. There has been a tendency in computer science to search for a universal computer – a magical AI bullet – to tackle all problems. This obsession has rather blinded computer scientists to the advantages of having many different tools. The greatest change in computing will come when multi-facility machines are built. In general, a specialist machine will always be faster at its range of tasks than a general-purpose machine; so a collection of semi-specialist machines combined with a general-purpose machine would tackle many tasks much faster. The problem is that it is not possible, in general, to analyse a task to see which machine should tackle it, or which aspect of a task should be tackled by each part of the mixed machine.

Thus we expect a new kind of parallel computer to develop – one that is heterogeneous in operation. It will contain many different sorts of processor, linked to each other by a complex back-plane on which chemical, electrical and optical signals can propagate in several different forms (analogue, digital, etc.). Each machine will be looking constantly at its inputs, trying to identify what it can do with them and placing the output on to the back-plane. It will monitor its own success – judged by others using its answers – and use this to refine how it tackles problems. Such a machine will exploit the parallel and serial interactions of its different processor elements, as well as the complex temporal dynamics imposed by the different speeds and effects of the back-plane message system to produce a whole new form of computation.

Such machines might use analogue properties to get a quick and rough answer before letting the digital machine refine its accuracy; or they might exploit the fast but inaccurate search of a quantum computer before confirming the answer by another means; or they might utilize the massively parallel pattern-matching ability of the chemical computer. Twenty-first-century computing will be fundamentally different as we move from the provable mathematical models of today to such mixed machines. In many ways they will emulate biology, where molecular, ionic and electronic effects on a range of time-scales give rise to the intelligent behaviour of animals.

Analogue Computing

The current world of computing and telecommunications has become totally digital, to the extent that to suggest an alternative is a form of heresy, to be ridiculed at all cost. Computing, however, has not always been digital, and there are good reasons to think that many forms of future computer may well have completely different characteristics: analogue, quantum and chemical computers are all very different from electronic digital machines. Many future applications may need the characteristics that these alternative computers offer. It is a key prediction of this chapter that in the future analogue computers will outnumber digital ones. The future is analogue!

The big drivers behind this different way of looking at computing will come as truly intelligent robots (rather than large mechanical pieces of equipment) and smart materials make their appearance. Robots use sensors and actuators that operate on the real world in complex, 'noisy' and non-linear fashions. It is very hard to match digital computing, which is designed for precise, accurate calculations, to this domain. Digital computers are inherently linear; all non-linearities have to be dealt with by simple linear sums that approximate to the actual effect. It becomes critical that the algorithm or program approximates sufficiently, or disaster can occur. Smart materials make the situation even worse. They respond to changes in the environment directly, not through some detached computational process. Linking their changes to a digital world will be difficult. Yet smart materials are the future. They will enable us to build self-regulating structures, miniature robots and a whole host of new devices that are currently very difficult to manufacture.

Digital computers were designed for exact solutions of mathematical equations. They are ideal for accountants and scientists. Engineers, on the other hand, are used to trying to build structures where precise calculations are very difficult due to their complexity. They are used to trying to control systems where accurate calculation of the best solution is either impossible or takes too long. For instance, in managing a major network the exact solution requires you to gather all the data together in one place, make a decision and then inform the sub-components how to act. By the time this has been done, the problem has changed and the original data is often noisy or corrupt. Analogue computing trades accuracy for speed, and in the future speed will be critical.

Analogue computing also allows the direct representation of non-linear problems. All difficult control and computational problems have non-linear elements in them. But analogue computing was largely abandoned because of noise problems in the components and an increasing interest in noise-free solutions. Modern electronics gets around many of the noise problems, however. There was also a belief that logical manipulation of 'symbols' was all that was needed to make a computer intelligent. The last fifty years of work in AI suggests that this may be a mistaken belief. Now almost all neural networks use artificially injected noise. It is possible that intelligence actually needs noise to prevent it getting trapped into logical pits. Thus analogue computing may be the only way forward.

A final key driver will be evolutionary computing, which is discussed later. Evolutionary computing needs analogue computers with a digital storage of genetic material and noise to demonstrate its true effectiveness. This is because evolution is more than just the accurate storage of information in DNA; it also requires a very complex mapping between what the DNA sequence is and its effect on the body of an organism. In biology, the folding and interaction of proteins 'translate' the stored DNA message into the physical structures on which evolution works – our bodies. The nearest analogy in computing is to use a digital storage to mimic the DNA and a (slightly noisy) analogue computer to mimic the complexity of the protein folding. Without both elements, evolutionary computing will struggle to have sufficient power to emulate the success of biology. Evolutionary computing will be the biggest difference between twenty-first-century ideas of the computer and how to program it, and today's computers. The need for analogue computers will grow with the realization that whole new fields will be opened up by evolutionary computing.

Robots, smart materials and intelligent systems that need noise, complex non-linear solutions and evolutionary computing will all eventually lead to a rethink of the idea that a single simple concept such as digital computing is sufficient for all problems. The twenty-first century will be too varied and complex for single-tool solutions. Analogue computing will come back in force.

Chips Everywhere
The chips-with-everything lifestyle is almost inevitable. Almost anything can be improved by adding some intelligence to it, and since the intelligence will be cheap to make, we will take advantage of this potential. In fact, smart ways of doing things are often

cheaper than dumb ways: a smart door lock, for instance, may be more economical to produce than a complex key-based lock. A chip is often cheaper than dumb electronics or electromechanics. However, the field of electronics no longer has a monopoly of chip technology. Some new chips incorporate tiny electromechanical or electrochemical devices to do jobs that used to be done by more expensive electronics. Chips now have the ability to analyse chemicals, biological matter or information. They are at home processing both atoms and bits.

The new families of chips have many possible uses; but since these chips are relatively new, most of their uses are probably still beyond our imagination. We have already seen the massive impact of chips on information-processing; we have much less intuition regarding their impact on the physical world.

Some chips have components that act as tiny pumps to allow drugs to be dispensed at exactly the right rate. Others have tiny mirrors that can control laser beams to make video displays. Gene chips have now been built that can identify the presence of many different genes, allowing applications from rapid identification to estimation of life expectancy for insurance reasons. (These chips are already being used to tell whether people have a genetic disorder so that their treatment can be determined correctly, and are speeding up genetic research).

It is easy to predict some of the uses that such future chips might have around the home and office, especially when they become disposable and cheap. Chips on fruit that respond to various gases may warn when the fruit is at its best, and when it should be discarded. Other foods might have electronic use-by dates that sound an alarm each time the cupboard or fridge is opened close to the end of their life. Other chips may detect the presence of moulds or harmful bacteria. Packaging chips may have embedded cooking instructions that communicate directly with the microwave, or may contain real-time recipes that appear on the kitchen terminal and tell the cook exactly what to do, and when. They might know what other foodstuffs are available in the kitchen, or whether they are in stock locally and at what price. Of course, these chips could also contain pricing and other information for use by the shops themselves, replacing bar codes and the like and allowing the customer to put all the products in a smart trolley and simply walk out, debiting their account automatically. Chips on food might react when another food is in close proximity, either warning the owner that there may be odour contamination, or advising him that the two could be combined well to make a particularly pleasant dish – cooking by numbers. In short, the kitchen could be a techno-utopia or a nightmare, depending on your point of view.

Simple sensors that switch on lights when a hand is waved nearby or when someone enters a room can already replace mechanical switches. In future, switches of all kinds will appear to have feelings – they may be rather more emotional, glowing, changing colour or shape, playing hide-and-seek, or creating a noise when a hand gets near, making them easier or more fun to use. They may respond initially to gestures or voice commands, but eventually they will infer what they are to do from something they pick up in conversation. Intelligent 'emotional' objects may become very commonplace. Many devices will act differently according to the person making the transaction. A security device might allow one person to enter, but phone the police if it detects a known burglar. Other people may receive a welcome message or be put in videophone contact with a resident, either in the house or away.

It will be possible to make devices burglar-proof by registering them in a home. They would continue to work while they were near various other fixed devices, maybe in the walls, but would not work when removed. The problem of moving home would be solved by broadcasting a digitally signed message to the chips. Air quality may be continuously analysed by chips, which would alert people to dangers such as carbon monoxide or excessive radiation, and these may also monitor for the presence of bacteria or viruses, or just pollen. They may be integrated into a home health system which could monitor our well-being on a variety of fronts, watching for stress, diseases, checking our blood pressure, fitness and so on. All of these health indicators could be monitored unobtrusively. The ultimate nightmare might be that our fridge would refuse to let us have any chocolate until the chips in our trainers have confirmed that we have done our exercise for the day.

Some chips in our home would be mobile, in robots, and would have a wide range of jobs, from cleaning and tidying to looking after the plants. Sensors in the soil may tell the robot exactly how much water and food the plant needs. Sensors on the stem or leaves may even monitor the plant itself.

The existing global positioning system already allows chips to know almost exactly where they are outside, and in-building positioning systems could eventually allow pinpointing to be millimetre precise. Position-dependent behaviour will therefore be commonplace. Similarly, events can be timed to the precision of atomic clock broadcasts. Response can be super-intelligent, adjusting appropriately for time, place, person, social circumstances, environmental conditions – anything that can be observed by any sort of sensor or predicted by any sort of algorithm. With this enormous versatility, it is very hard to think of anything where some sort of chip could not make an improvement. The ubiquity of the chip will depend on how fast costs fall and how valuable a certain task is, but we will eventually have chips in everything.

Once we do have chips in everything, the limitations to today's software systems will be overwhelmingly apparent. Already it is difficult to predict what will happen when you plug two large and complex systems together. Imagine what will happen when all the electronic devices in the world have the potential to talk to each other, and work by sampling the noisy uncertainties of the physical world. A completely new paradigm of operation is needed.

Firstly, such systems will need to talk to each other in a flexible, universal language. Since one of the advantages of chips in everything is the potential to replace mechanical control systems with the spoken word, it would be natural for devices to speak to each other in the same language as is used for controlling devices. After all, American English is likely to be the most common commercial language, and we are far more familiar with it than any hypothetical new language. Thus all devices will probably have an 'American language' API (an interface that allows programs to link with or control features in a system). At least then they will all know what they are saying to each other – all they will have to agree is the rate of talking.

Secondly, since chips will need to adapt to new devices and patterns of behaviour, they are likely to be built on the principle that each device acts as an intelligent agent with a bounded ability to learn and to change its behaviours. Finally, there will need to be a way of creating an operating system that is simple at one level, open-ended and flexible. The only solution would be to treat all the intelligent agent devices as static examples of the ANT system. Indeed, treating all the chips as components of one great ant nest may be a very interesting way of visualizing how they will work together, each with its own special role in the colony. Such a collection of devices would be able to try to find novel solutions through self-organization, and to carry out repair when one of its number went wrong.

Chips in everything will be much more than just a cheap way to get more-intelligent control. Used correctly, they will change completely the communication and computing environment.

Network Computers and the Smart Badge

There has been a great deal of debate in the last couple of years over the place of network computers (NCs). The current devices are basically PCs without disk drives. They download their software and information across the network each time they are switched on. This means that they can be made slightly cheaper and lighter than full PCs. However, both the price of PCs and the size and weight of disk-drive PCs have dropped so fast that net-PCs are now in the frame, making the most of their own local storage and processing, and using remote network stores for longer-term document and software storage. Both of these systems have their place, as do full-blown PCs, but the argument really misses the point. The fact is that, with a decent network, the only thing you need with you is an interface. With this, both processing and storage are available remotely. This means that you can work from anywhere and have full access to all the files, programs and information that you have from your desk. In fact, this way of working is feasible whether PC, NC, net-PC or any other arrangement is used, provided the source is accessible to the network.

The interface with the network could be based on something as simple and as compact as a smart badge, or some other similarly sized device in a handbag. Access could be voice based: you might simply touch the smart badge and say, 'Give me the file I was working on last night' or 'Read me my e-mail'. The voice would travel over the mobile network to a remote computer, which could then read the file into your earphone, or display it on your eyepiece. This eyepiece may be a pair of spectacles with a projector and mirror to give a virtual screen, or ultimately an active contact lens, allowing full three-dimensional overlays on the real world – *Robocop*-style information. Getting information into the computer could again be voice based, or a variety of other tools may be used. Air-typing and air-mice are possible, with a camera watching your fingers and the remote computer analysing the image to determine what you are doing. This type of smart badge could of course have many other functions, helping security, as an ego badge, electronic cash store, and health monitor, to name just a few uses.

III

MATERIALS AND DEVICES

The Ego Badge

A few years ago, we were looking at uses for cordless communication based on infrared, and other people were developing smart badges for access to computers and buildings, for tracking and so on. We had the idea that the badge could hold lots of personal information about the holder as well as boring security and access stuff. When two badge-wearers met, the badges would exchange information. At first, they would swap fairly superficial details, then if various criteria were met, they might release more. Provided both badges agreed, they would then warn their owners.

This could have simple business uses, such as finding someone at an airport or swapping business-card details. More interestingly, they could have social uses. They could be loaded with information on hobbies and interests, age, religion and, more realistically, sexual preferences, since it quickly became obvious that the main market for such devices would be in nightclubs. When you bump into your ideal partner, lights might flash and romantic music might play, saving you hours of dancing with all the wrong people. The idea was greeted with laughter and scorn by some of our colleagues. But, apparently, the designers at Philips had thought of exactly the same idea, to the last function. The only difference seems to be that they called theirs 'Hot Badges'. It does not matter which of us was first; this sort of thing happens all the time – we are all exposed to similar information and it is very common to think of the same idea at the same time. At least someone is running with it. The badges could use infrared, radio or ultrasound – each has its merits, but infrared would not work if the badge were in a lady's handbag, or hidden behind clothing. Such badges will doubtless evolve and will eventually work in conjunction with ear-pieces, eyepieces and, eventually, active contact lenses.

Smart Clothing

The military have experimented with some interesting new types of clothing over the last few years. One development involves clothes that can change their thickness, and therefore their thermal properties, according to the outside temperature; another involves splashing medicines on to a wound when a soldier is hit by a bullet. Optical fibres can be woven into the clothes so that when a soldier is injured, the fibres are broken and information about the wound is relayed to field medics, who can then prioritize casualties. Obviously, other sensors could monitor blood loss, pulse, etc., and this information could also be relayed to medics.

Millions of microcapsules can be built into clothing to allow camouflage to adapt dynamically to the surroundings by changing the colour and pattern of the clothes. Such effects can be achieved in a variety of ways, using electrical charge or physical pressure. Today's high-tech camouflage technology may eventually become street fashion, with kaleidoscopic clothing.

But screen technology is moving on, too, and manufacturers are not far from producing flexible polymer screens that could be built into clothes. Imagine a T-shirt which has a video display panel where the logo should be. Instead of static prints, you could walk around showing video clips, perhaps from a TV tuner on your belt, or you could show accompanying videos while dancing to music at a nightclub. Smaller panels could be built into sleeves or legs. You could have a wristwatch in your shirtsleeve.

As plastic conductors become commonplace over the next few years, a wide variety of flexible gadgetry can be built into clothes – cellphones, radios, diaries, shopping terminals, electronic cash, identification chips, even computers. Communications between the various devices could use fibres built into clothes, but that would limit their coverage to a single garment, unless connectors were used to link garments together. Another technique transmits signals through the body at surprisingly high data rates, possibly as much as several megabits per second.

Sensor technology will allow clothes to monitor health. A modified wristwatch is already available that can record a heartbeat for thirty seconds and download the recording through a telephone to the hospital. Of course, such devices could be built into a shirt to record the heart all day and to signal the hospital immediately if anything were amiss. Doctors would thus be able to monitor patients carefully without keeping them in hospital. Wearable devices to monitor blood pressure, blood-sugar level, stress and many other health indicators will all become much more common than today. We may even see monitors for mental activity and emotional state.

Body suits are already used for virtual-reality-based applications, using sensors all over the body to detect movements. Vibration and pressure devices can be used to output information to the wearer. Someday, maybe as early as 2015, wearable electronics will be able to link directly to peripheral nerves to produce tactile sensations. In conjunction with appropriate displays and earphones, immersive applications could become almost indistinguishable from reality – just like on the Schwarzenegger film *Total Recall*.

Power supply is a big problem today, since battery technology has not progressed at the same rate as other information technologies. But manufacturers of mobile-telephone equipment have mastered a number of tricks. Low-power chips, battery-management and power-management systems, low-power reflective light displays, and even shoes that can generate electricity have all been invented. We may soon see common use of fuel cells and possibly solar power, maybe, again, even built into clothing. We have to hope that development is swift, or we may be carrying around a rucksack full of batteries.

Smart Materials

There are a number of key developments that will differentiate the twenty-first century from the twentieth; but if someone from the twentieth century were to travel into the future, it would be smart materials that would disorientate him the most. Indeed, smart materials will change the way we do so many things that it is impossible to analyse their full impact here. Quite simply, in this brief discussion we are bound to miss many of the things that will become important, and gloss the significance of the few that we do mention.

A smart material is defined as one that alters its properties as a result of changes in the environment in a manner that an outside observer would deem to be both useful and 'intelligent' rather than reactive. There are many simple and advanced examples of how smart materials could work. Materials that contract strongly when a weak electric field is applied could be used to form artificial muscles; windows that change their opacity according to the heat of the building could form part of a self-regulating environment; and small vesicles that leak drugs when they contact the target organism or cell could be used in medicine. All smart materials share a common set of features: they react in a fairly complex, self-regulating and local way to changes in the environment. Thus they remove the necessity to have complex control systems, sensors and actuators. Smart materials are a natural partner to developments such as nano-robotics and analogue computing. It is the combination of these technologies that will lead to great strides in the use of robots and in changing medical practice.

Microbots – New World Creatures

A lot of research is under way to develop small robots that resemble insects. There are already hybrids, such as cockroaches that have had their wings replaced by an electronic interface to a remote-control system and that can be forced to go in any direction. Such robots and hybrids are being designed for a variety of purposes, mostly noble and benign, and early imagined uses include crop pollination, guiding swarms of full biological insects to fields to enable pollination, or luring real insects to their deaths to control populations.

However, another obvious use is in industrial espionage, where a robotic insect might transport miniaturized surveillance equipment into a competitor's office and then listen or look in on activities. These may come and go entirely unnoticed by the human inhabitants or intruder warning systems. Such devices could help a lot in identifying the physical location of cyberspace opponents.

Another use of these devices may be in sabotage, and they would work well as part of the weaponry in a cyberwar, crossing the boundary into physical conflict. In most computer systems, security prevents or controls infection by viruses, either by stopping software from entering the machine by blocking floppy access, or by stopping software which has already entered the machine from corrupting files or erasing hard disks, etc. However, an insect-sized robot could gain physical access to the computer's internal devices directly. Homing in on the hard-disk interface, for example, the drive could be disabled or erased, or data could be copied or manipulated without the operator finding out. The whole machine could be sabotaged in the same way, by shorting out circuits or by killing off chips with static shocks. These devices are in their infancy at the moment in the civilian world, but development could be swift, and we cannot be sure how far off these possibilities lie, or even whether the military already have such a capability.

In their current form, these microbots undoubtedly occupy only physical space, but future versions may straddle the boundary between physical space and cyberspace. They may have physical bodies, but the fact that they can interact directly with electronic devices offers scope for an extension to their existence. Interfacing to the electronic domain allows part of their existence to be in cyberspace. They may not need a physical brain, but could have this stored remotely. Their 'mind' may be in cyberspace, but their body could be in the physical domain. It would be as if a cyberspace creature had been given real-world existence and senses.

We must consider whether this model extends to any robot, and, if so, does it make any difference if the 'brain' or 'mind' is part of that body or not? We think that it can be either. The robot may be thought of as having its own 'mental space', and this could either be isolated and individual in the true sense or a fully integral part of cyberspace. Although there is a difference, the distinction between the two may be philosophical, with no real significance for us.

IV

EVOLUTION

Artificial Evolution

There are a number of essential developments that will change our whole perception of the function of computing and telecommunications. Clearly, this includes the nature and amount of computing power available, and the potential applications that this power could have when allied with the tremendous amount of bandwidth that optical fibres will bring. However, there are changes much more profound in software and the control of systems that will challenge two of the very things that we believe distinguish us from mere machines: autonomy and evolution. In the next few sections we will examine what will happen in the coming two decades as the power of evolution is harnessed to the raw information-processing power of the computer. Artistic creativity, software programming, the ability to understand systems – all will be handed over to machines.

Artificial evolution is very simple in essence. You begin with a population of individuals, and then apply a test or environment that results in some doing better than others. The poorer performers tend to die; the better ones, to reproduce. Those that reproduce pass on (in digital form) their 'genetic material'; that is, some expression of how to build them. And you repeat the exercise many times over.

The techniques of artificial evolution all mimic to a greater or lesser extent ideas from biology. They have been applied to evolving software, hardware designs, chemical structures, music, pictures and video. Although there are advantages in certain methods of computing the outcome, they all share a common result: a human has not designed the final product. The nearest that is achieved is when a user is responsible for selecting which individuals survive; normally this is used only to amplify artistic criteria.

Evolution produces solutions that we do not necessarily comprehend; it places an emphasis on robust solutions and adaptability; and, in theory, it is computationally more powerful than programming a computer. Yet evolution is feared for taking computers into realms where people can neither understand them nor trust them. Frequently, evolved programs are rejected as somehow unreliable, and a human is used instead. This is probably the most ironic of all possible misunderstandings of technology. Evolution will be a major tool of the future. Just as computers will break free of the need for people to understand them, so evolution will drive the process. Ultimately, the evolution of the human race will also become artificial and change our very future.

Evolving Hardware

Hardware design has traditionally been done by hand, and more recently with computer-aided design and optimization. Because the circuits designed are so complex, various engineering practices are used to make the projects manageable. For instance, designs are repeated across the chip or copied from libraries. Various 'bottlenecks' emerge as ways of controlling the complexity. Systems are built so that the timing of control signals is precisely regulated. All of these techniques make the problem easier, but they significantly reduce the power of the deployed hardware. Furthermore, if the hardware's purpose changes so that it goes beyond the original design specification, or if it is damaged, then it must be redesigned or replaced.

By way of contrast, most biological organisms have managed to squeeze the maximum performance from noisy, complex systems without constant problems. They seem to thrive on and exploit timing delays and parasitic currents. This appears to be a feature of biology's design process – evolution. Could the same approach be used to build the next generation of hardware and thus squeeze more performance from every square centimetre of silicon?

Two developments point the way to a very different hardware future. The first is the growth of FPGAs (field programmable gate arrays) and EPACs (electronically programmable analogue circuits).

Both of these were designed so that engineers could test their ideas before a production run, but increasingly it is possible to rewrite the chip configuration in operation. So, for instance, a processor could optimize its design for the problem in hand. However, a specialist processor beats a general purpose one every time, since it is optimized for a specific task, so a processor that spends the first few clock cycles reconfiguring to the best structure will, on many big problems, be the best application of the technology. We can imagine a very different computer in the future that continuously shapes itself to the problem.

This is just the beginning, however. The second development will be the use of evolutionary techniques to change the wiring pattern of the FPGA so that it is optimized for the program that is running. Currently a human designer selects the way the logic elements are wired and how this is used to change the FPGA's function. Imagine that as a program was running it monitored its own performance and used this to try new wiring patterns till it found the optimal one. The machine could evolve its own internal wiring to achieve its tasks. This has already been demonstrated. A chip evolved the best method of separating two frequencies by measuring its own success and using this to select progressively better designs. The resulting wiring diagram bore no relation to those designed by humans. Parts of the chip that were not even wired into the main signal pathway contributed to the device's performance. Evolution exploits many more effects and much more of the physics than restrictive design practices allow. The result was a chip that used about a quarter of the gates a human designer would have needed. In the future, chips designed this way will be much more powerful than hand-built ones.

Another curious feature emerged, unshackled by the need to fit engineering practice: it was almost impossible to understand how the resulting circuit functioned. Unlike evolving software, which often uses a man-made look-up table to check its results, the hardware's performance resulted from the direct feedback of the efficiency with which it separated two signals. With no *a priori* knowledge built in, it was difficult to dissect the circuit into functional components. Such systems in the future will not be understood at a functional level by the builders – only that they produce the desired results. This appears to worry many, and yet it is no different, in essence, than trusting a person to perform a job. We do not understand how people work, we merely observe to our satisfaction that they do so.

Evolving hardware will again challenge our precepts about machines and people. Such machines will reconfigure to the task, design their internal workings in opaque manners, and require us to trust their operation rather than their design. They will feel like living machines.

Evolving Software

A key feature of the Industrial Revolution was the replacement of hand-crafted manufacture with mass-production techniques. In the early period of industrialization, craftsmen used machines as tools of manufacture; later the machines completely supplanted the craftsman. Computer development has reached a similar stage in its development: the computer is a tool used by a skilled programmer to produce an end product – a program. Software engineering is still a craftsman's industry, awaiting the development of mass production. With the advent of evolutionary software, the equivalent transformation may be about to take place and move programming from a professional skill to an everyday event.

Computers were designed to be programmed by programmers. In the 1980s it was shown that any programmable computer could not learn or evolve well. For a computer to be easily programmed, it must be obvious when a mistake has been made. One of the consequences of this is that if one were to generate random sequences of computer instructions, almost none of them would work. Programming is rather like walking a tightrope: it requires high skill and a careful touch! In contrast, evolving systems must work for most possible cases, the result being that the solutions generated are never simply 'right' or 'wrong'. This is a more natural state of affairs for people. Outside mathematics and bank accounts, total accuracy is seldom required – a 'good enough' answer will normally do. 'Good enough' computing will be the watchword of the twenty-first century.

Evolving software mimics biological evolution with collections of programs competing with each other to see which performs the task best. The better ones breed to produce offspring and to drive the process further. Computer programs can already be bred that tackle small, complex tasks and produce results difficult for programmers to understand. However, their full beauty will be realized only when we move away from digital computing to evolvable hardware or analogue computing, domains where the evolutionary techniques are ideally suited. By 2010 it is possible that many programs will contain impenetrable, evolved code, and by 2020 the vast majority will be only evolved code.

A simple scenario for that time will be that people buy a code generator for their home appliances that will generate programs to shape the appliances' functions to the user as a result of interacting with him. Formal methods for transforming natural-language requests to code, libraries of starting points, and shared information with other evolving agents on other appliances will all speed the procedure up. The individual will own the personalized software.

The software industry will therefore undergo a profound change. Instead of making large amounts of money duplicating bits of information, it will be reduced to providing better evolutionary systems that enable people to grow their own code. The role of a software company will be akin to that of the tractor manufacturer to the farmer. Mass production of personalized code will take a different form from the mass production of manufactured goods, but it will change the industry just as profoundly.

V

INTERFACES

Active Contact Lens Interface

One boring afternoon back in 1991, we were discussing virtual reality (VR) and how cumbersome the new headset was. We could not imagine it ever being a success with such a heavyweight helmet. No one would use it if they thought they looked silly, especially when they could not see other people's expressions when they were wearing it. What was needed was a much lighter and unobtrusive affair. We wondered whether it might be possible to do the same thing using glasses or contact lenses. With a pair of glasses, a small laser could write a beam directly on to the retina, and this could be powered and controlled easily via wires built into the glasses. This seemed too low-tech; there had to be a way of fitting everything into a one-centimetre lens. With ongoing miniaturization in semiconductor technology, it is only a matter of time before the receiver and processing circuitry could be built into the periphery of such a lens. A few phone calls later we confirmed that surface-emitting lasers would eventually come down to the size and efficiency required. Initially, we had thought of using a large array of such lenses, one for each pixel, and we put the date when sufficient miniaturization could be expected at around 2030, at least. Another big problem we had to deal with was how the beams from the lasers would be focused, originating as they did so close to the eyeball. Nonetheless, the preliminary design was there, and we had forty years to solve the other problems.

The lens would be made of diamond, already on the horizon as a wonder material of the early twenty-first century. It would offer protection from excess heat as well as from nasty chemicals. The power could come either from induction, using body heat, or even from remote infrared powering. Most of the processing would be done remotely, signalling to the lens via a radio link. To an observer, the lasers would be too small to be individually visible so it would resemble just an ordinary tinted lens. Using liquid crystal display (LCD) technology in the lens, the lens could switch vision of the outside world on or off, by making the lens opaque or transparent, or offer an overlay of VR on the real world. Having listed this as a great idea that we would have to wait for ever to achieve, it was put on the shelf. But one day we read that arrays of micro-mirrors had been invented for use in reflecting or deflecting an incoming laser beam to make a TV picture, which struck us as a brilliant idea. These mirrors could toggle only between two positions, but by the time the other lens components are ready the mirrors will be much more sophisticated. The only remaining problem of principle was focusing. Beams from the original array of tiny lasers would have diverged enormously and the focusing problem seemed insurmountable, but with micro-mirrors we could steer the beams from just a few lasers so they could be much bigger. Also, we could mount them transversely in the lens thereby getting several millimetres of focusing length. At last! So we had the final design. We now think the basic components of an active contact lens will be around in about 2008, twenty years earlier than our original estimate. Whether anyone ever builds one is another matter. While lightweight spectacles doing the same job could be handed around a group and would require lower technology, there seem to be few major advantages of the lens approach. But there are some. Firstly, it would be much less obvious that anyone was wearing them. Imagine walking around a strange town, with a huge arrow superimposed on your field of view showing you which way to go to your destination. Imagine that as you walk past a shop, some images tell you there is a sale on that camera you were dreaming of. Then as you approach someone, you see *Robocop*-style information all about them, relayed from a network based on the images being captured by the video circuitry in the lens. Imagine the social embarrassment you could avoid when they greet you and you have no idea who they are. Now the information is all there in front of you. In a business meeting, imagine the advantage when your computer back at base is listening in to the conversation and sending you information to assist you.

With two such contact lenses, three-dimensional full immersion is simple. Virtual reality can be that much more convincing when the user is freed from the headset. It will become possible to wander freely round a convincing three-dimensional environment, just like the holodeck on the science-fiction programme *Star Trek*.

But all of this pales into insignificance compared with one major advantage. With a clumsy VR headset, you can go to the virtual office without leaving the comfort of your own bed. With an active contact lens, you won't even have to open your eyes!

Holodecks

Many of us have wished we could have holodecks today. During our leisure time, we could describe our fantasy to the computer, which would then create it for us with synthesized people and places with whom and with which we could interact. The computer would be able to fill in the detail and make intelligent guesses as to the sorts of people and objects to use as padding. So, we may suggest a mid-twentieth-century New York detective's office and 'some kind of mystery to solve' and the computer would oblige, with an environment, activities and people indistinguishable from reality.

Most of the technology will become available in the next twenty years. A small room may be completely lined with high-resolution three-dimensional displays, or a user may wear active contact lenses for the visual input. We already know how to produce a sound anywhere in three-dimensional space. With these technologies alone we would be able to wander round and explore a synthesized environment. In just a couple of decades, the computer will be fast enough and smart enough to drive it reasonably convincingly too, so the environment would look and sound lifelike. For leisure, entertainment, education and teletravel it would already be acceptable.

But that is not all. Perhaps by 2015, and certainly by 2020 on today's projections, we should be able to make inputs directly into the peripheral nervous system. This means that we can dispense with the cumbersome data gloves of today but have a more realistic sense of touch in the virtual environment – probably smell and taste, too, making the experience even more convincing and compelling.

There is one other emerging technology that may go the whole way. With the promise of nano-technology on the distant horizon, at least one visionary has suggested how we could build the fluid 'liquid metal' matter used in the T1000 terminator from the Schwarzenegger movie *Terminator 2*. Robodyne Systems has already demonstrated the basic principle, albeit on a much bigger physical scale. It constructed a robot out of cubes that can slide over each other along every surface. Each cube is able to hold specific tools and to carry out specific functions. Thus, the robot can rearrange itself into any structure subject to the number and sizes of the cubes. But then there is the clever bit. Each cube is made of smaller ones, and these can be made of smaller ones still. Using this principle, Joe Michael, who created the concept at Robodyne Systems, envisages a distant future where an entire building – the walls and the furniture – could be one of these fractal shape-changing robots. He suggests that a real holodeck with real reconfigurable matter could also be built. Once the size of the blocks gets down to micron levels, almost any texture, look and feel could be produced. Add some computing and sensory capability and you have a T1000 robot that can change into any shape at will. But don't forget to program it with Asimov's laws of robotics, please! Since routine mechanical nano-technology and the ability to produce micron-size movable cubes could be with us by 2020, around the same time as smarter-than-man machines, we can expect very rapid development thereafter.

The very long-term future involves direct links between the brain and computers – real *Total Recall* stuff – expected sometime after 2030. This could in principle create an environment that was completely indistinguishable from reality. Much of this idea has been explored in science fiction already, but we really must think about the consequences for those who may find it all too compelling to spend most of their spare time in synthetic worlds and shared spaces, far away from reality.

Living Interfaces

Imagine yourself sitting in front of a computer in the year 2020. What do you see? Most people expect windows, icons, some pointing device and slightly better graphics. Perhaps it will be 'easier' to use. But twenty years is an eternity in the computing business. In 1980 personal computers were just beginning to make an appearance, with line editors or, that joy of users, full-screen editors. Commands were typed out in full to tell the machine how to act. All that icons did was replace the typing with a button. Files and folders copied all the frustrations of a paper-based filing system (where do you put a document and how do you find it?) with the electronic equivalent. If there was ever an example of the first use of a new technology copying the old, this was it! If by 2020 we are still using our computers in such a way then we will have wasted their power.

By then, computers will have the raw information-processing power of the human brain, or very close to it. They will also be able to adapt and learn. They will be able to speak and listen reasonably. They will be connected to millions of machines around the world by ultra-fast links. It is likely that the computer will have 'disappeared' into the environment as a result of there being chips in everything. In fact, chips will be so cheap that it will be easier to build a toaster with a voice interface than to build it with buttons. Buttons will be considered as 'retro' as wind-up watches are today, and devices with buttons on them will be bought by people either as an aggressive Luddite statement or as a reminder of times past.

Furthermore, the idea that our computer is an inanimate object which sits at home or is lugged around in a briefcase will appear wonderfully old-fashioned. We will expect its persona to track us wherever we go. Our computer will be a virtual thing. The key technologies that are needed to deliver this can be grouped under a single heading – living interfaces. Here we will try to track the development of these interfaces through some of their possible steps.

Firstly, intelligent agents will become ubiquitous. Not because there is anything intelligent about them yet, but because they represent a different way of thinking about how to interact with systems. They break the problem down into tasks that could be managed by a human, and are built around ideas of negotiation and personalization which are much more natural to deal with.

The next step will come when it is understood that people are emotional beings; we need our systems to attune to our mood. Such agents will concentrate not on what we are doing but on how we are doing it. They will use tone of voice, facial expressions, speed of typing and error rates to sense our prevailing mood, in much the same way that a pet does. Cameras and microphones, which before long will be prevalent on PCs, will enable this richer world of emotional cues to be exploited by the machine. Finally, the computer will come of age as a helper.

Once this step has been mastered, the understanding of language will be much easier, as so much of language is 'unspoken' or hidden in the tones and expressions. The living interface will be able to learn the subtleties of language when it can recognize the mood of the user. In turn, it will be able to use tone, expression (through synthetic faces) and words to create its own living persona.

Around the same time, the presence of chips in almost every device – and the replacement of dials and knobs with voice interfaces – will make communicating with our computer persona easy. There will no longer be a need to carry a communication device. The whole world will communicate with you, and your computer persona will track your presence. Speak and your friend will be present. The concept of not being tracked by the computer, of being out of touch, will be as difficult for people to grasp as the idea of renouncing one's own identity: it will be meaningless. As for the location of the computer running your persona, that, too, will be a strange question. It is like asking where is the air that enables you to breathe. The persona will run on an appliance that enables it to express itself near you.

This will be a totally different form of interface from the world of communication and computing – an intelligent, emotional agent whose sole desire is to help you. Available at a second's notice wherever you travel, it will become an indispensable tool early in the twenty-first century.

PART II

THE IMPACT OF
TECHNOLOGY

Introduction

Change is a natural characteristic of our lives: we may get married, have children, move house or change job, to name but a few significant events; the fashion industry is driven by biannual fads about how we look; politicians change their philosophies and principles every time they enter office. Technological change, however, is less blatant, more insidious, more gradual and more effective. At this juncture in history there is a big debate about which technology will have the most profound effect: information technology, materials science or biotechnology? Like many such debates, drawing lines and treating items in isolation misses a key point: all of these technologies will converge, as telecommunications and computing are already doing. The result of that convergence will be as profound on the world around us, and on the way we look at ourselves, as if we had been visited by extra-terrestrials. Arthur C. Clarke put it very nicely when he said, 'future technology is indistinguishable from magic'; we, from our current position of little knowledge or wisdom, can barely see this magical and strange future. More technological change will take place in the next century than has occurred in the period from the dawn of cities till now. Only one thing will not change: our social needs.

Within a decade, some of today's industries will be dead. Prime candidates are those in the 'middleman' role. Computer programs under the control of the end customers will replace these. If your job title contains the word 'agent', it is at risk now. Intelligent computer assistants will boost productivity and even act creatively. Already computers are beginning to produce music as good as leading jazz musicians. New industries will arise where the penetration of mechanical assistance and computer intelligence is less important. These will be the 'caring' industries, where human contact and touch is critical. We will move beyond the information economy and into the care economy, before many people have realized it even exists.

The nature of work will change profoundly. Jobs will typically be short; job changes will be frequent; and companies will consist of a small core of key staff and many short-term or teleworking contractors. Telework will expand, as it will permit people to chase jobs round the globe and still live where they desire. A side-effect of this internationalization of jobs will be the strengthening of local communities, as people will spend much more time in one physical place, with less stressful commuting and deeper roots.

Many companies will be truly global, with workers on every continent, picked specifically for the task in hand. But we will still have numerous small and local companies – there are as many factors pushing this way as there are towards multinationals. However, the nature of companies will change as virtual-company technologies will make it just as easy for contractors to group together into virtual cooperatives. As a consequence, the balance between employee and employer will probably shift towards the employee. Both, however, will have more choices open to them.

The computer and communications network will change the look of our homes as well. Flat screens hanging on walls will reconfigure themselves according to our mood and the latest fashion to show real-life images or works of art. Art will move from the static to exploit fully dynamic, changing images. Coffee mornings with friends on distant continents shared through life-size videophone images; robot servants doing simple household chores; self-cleaning materials; and insect robots tending your garden – all will become commonplace in the next twenty-five years. Many people will replace pets with lifelong electronic companions capable of all the emotional responses of a pet but without the nuisances, or the misery of its departure. Such pets will be fully animated robots, in constant communication with the outside world in order to serve you.

Entertainment will expand beyond computer games, or simple three-dimensional or VR images. Robotic cubes that can reconfigure themselves into different structures could lead us to entertainment environments similar to the holodeck seen on *Star Trek*. The growing ability of artificial intelligence in limited domains means that some of the characters will be independent computer programs rather than other people. Friends will be able to visit us in our own special space, from anywhere on the globe. Perhaps we will eventually have more friends abroad than locally, which, we hope, may reduce some of the international misunderstandings and stereotypes. However, with computer people, the ability to pretend to be someone else remotely or to swap gender will add a piquancy to our relationships not present today. Computer-aided relations will be far from dull!

No VR experience will ever replace the need to see and to touch the real thing. Indeed, just as photography and films stimulate the desire to travel, VR will probably increase travel even more. Some of the great barriers to travel – trying to organize all the details and getting a package suited to oneself – will vanish as computer agents arrange it all for us. Strangers will be less intimidating, as intelligent badges will swap information that helps you find a compatible person. Active contact lenses worn in the eye and in contact with a network will inform us of phrases and social etiquette, enabling even the most socially inept to avoid mistakes.

The increase in socialization and working with people from other countries will change our society gradually. New power structures will emerge. We will become more focused and loyal to either our local community where we have chosen to live or to our segment of the global community with whom we have chosen to interact. National governments will have much less influence. Cybercommunities, organizing themselves rapidly in response to slow central governments will be very influential. Members of such communities would be anonymous, making defence difficult: tribalism can be very effective on a network.

We will see local-community networks growing rapidly, supporting all manner of activities and providing information and help. Teletourism will enable people to see if a locality is attractive to them, and will enable local museums and galleries to flourish through the generation of cyber-revenues.

Governments will have to adapt or become irrelevant. As communities become less based on geographic or political boundaries, nation states will decline along with their tax base. Many companies will process and sell information, which is not confined by borders. These companies may contain no human employees at all, and may exist transiently on any one movable computer. They could roam around the global network, staying in each country for just a few minutes at a time. Where would such a company be taxed and regulated? Taxing physical goods would be the easy option, but their decreasing proportion of the national income would make doing so a liability rather than an asset. It would be equivalent to a modern government taxing only land (i.e. agriculture) because it could not tax physical goods or services.

Computer- and robot-linked surveillance, the prevalence of cameras on many pieces of equipment, and the use of automatic face, fingerprint and voice recognition will all change the nature of security. The problem will be a feeling of invasiveness. Number-plate recognition, speed cameras, iris-scanners (people can be uniquely identified by their irises; some security systems already use iris-scanning, and this could become commonplace) and other surveillance measures will mean that we will be watched all the time. Do we accept the benefits; do we feel frightened by Big Brother; or do we regulate him? The choices will be very complex and hard.

A great deal of change has occurred over the last ten years. All the signs we can see suggest that the rate of change is increasing. The future could be very exciting and enjoyable as the technologies make the world a safer place with a high quality of life for all. Alternatively, we could hoard our gains and keep them for a few, reject them or use them to try to control others. History generally shows that technology has been abused – but also that few people would give up the advances we now enjoy. It is our decision, and with it goes the responsibility to ensure the best outcomes are achieved by forging on in an informed, intelligent and caring fashion.

I

THE IMPACT OF INTELLIGENT AGENTS

Brands and Agents

How will shops protect their brand images in such a world? Doubtless, some of the big brands will have the size needed to guarantee that people will want them in their personal worlds even without the choice to customize their image. Those trademarks will survive the longest. Others will have to fall in line quickly or see their market share disappear as people just ignore them and use other brands which allow customers to decide. New ways of establishing brands will come into existence in the struggle for survival, and the simple logo or trademark might be reduced in importance.

Of course, for shopping and similar activities, much or even most of the work will be done by agents. These will wander round, looking for the best deals, negotiating and sorting out shortlists, before bringing back the appropriate details to be visualized and presented to the user in his own personal world. Agents themselves are not particularly impressed by brands, unless specifically told by the user to prefer some brands to others. The agent might know to prefer Sony to Panasonic even if the other terms are the same, but would care nothing about their trademarks or site styles. Sites that are agent-friendly, provide information and negotiate happily will be at least considered in a search. Others which insist on customers' visiting their sites personally will see their revenue fall sharply.

In this agent-dominated world, brands will be quickly disassociated with visual trademarks, since people will rarely see them. The abstract qualities of a brand (reliability, quality, associated lifestyle, etc.) will survive, and if the brand is perceived by users to be sufficiently better than its competitors, or if people are still exposed via other media to advertising about the brand, it will continue to have a place in the network market; that is, so long as people care enough to assign a value to it or to tell their agents to prefer it.

However, it is not all bad news for brands. As agents search the convenient universe for suitable products in the right price range, etc., people will be faced with more choice, as competing products are increasingly forced to offer exactly the same deals. Bewilderment will result, and we will see many people making final decisions based on trust of particular brands, just like some do now. Nevertheless, it will initially be a more dynamic market-place with brands rising and falling on the basis of trusted recommendation spreading quickly across the net. What might be seen as best and sell like hot cakes today, might be found lacking by a trusted reviewer tomorrow and another brand will take the lead. Agents might well be instructed to check reviews automatically as part of a search. Instead of relying on Nike or Ford, or any other existing brand, people will depend more on the reviewers, who will become increasingly important and will be the new brands. An example from supermarkets illustrates what will happen. Sainsbury's own-brand products are made by a range of manufacturers, but carry the 'Sainsbury' label as a guarantee of reasonable quality at less than top-of-the-market price. People trust the label and buy many of the store's own-brand products in preference to well-established traditional brands. The same applies in Tesco with its own brand. Although Sainsbury and Tesco may never try the experiment, their own brands would probably sell quite well in the other's stores.

In cyberspace, this will happen to a greater extent. Traditional brands will suffer in the face of classifications by trusted review companies. People will decide how far up market they want to buy, or will want products to fit a particular lifestyle, and there will be companies that define which products fit those categories of quality, price, lifestyle, or whatever. These review companies – essentially quality guarantors – will be the hotel guides and consumer maga-zines of the Internet, but they will have much greater significance. They will also be the new brands, horizontal across a wide range of products, totally independent of either shops or manufacturers.

This branding will apply not only to industrial-age products, but to information, too. Sites will guarantee the quality of the information available from their links, and these might become the Yahoos of the future. More probably, Yahoo and the other directories and search engines will start doing this themselves.

Retailing and Agents

While brands will find the world changing rapidly, retailers will be caught completely unprepared. Their existing business plans presume a site on the net where people can visit their shop. But they do not take account of a world where people create a shortlist on the net, try things on in town, and then buy their choice from the best or cheapest supplier with a single button click on their personal digital assistant (PDA) or cellphone. In this world, some shops will be reduced to being little more than factory showrooms. They may make very few sales in the actual shop, especially if people can get a 30 per cent discount at the touch of a button by electronically purchasing direct from the manufacturer. It may even become possible to narrow down the selection from home, have the entire shortlist shipped to the door, and return just the rejects. Obviously, having a direct link to the manufacturer also increases the market for customized products, too. All of this will greatly increase the size of the distribution sector.

With people having the ability to buy the cheapest products, while still having all the choice and advice, it is difficult to see how retailing can survive in its current form. The pain will be reduced by this not happening overnight, but in the long term it seems inevitable. Most shopping will eventually be in cyberspace, between customer and manufacturer, with advice from third parties. There will be no wholesaling, no retailing, only service and distribution.

However, just because shops and retailing will be fundamentally changed, this does not mean that the other aspects of shopping cannot still make money. By offering attractive virtual environments, catering for the social and leisure sides of shopping, and by providing side services such as advice, agents, simple purchasing and funds transfer, guarantees and assured quality of service, there is still much money to be made in this industry – it is just that it will be made by different organizations.

Self-Configuring and Living Ads

The goal of all advertisers is to convince you, and very personally you, to buy their product. Most advertising works by trying to get emotional buy-in; occasionally, by providing information. However, the media used is far from ideal for either purpose. Newspapers and magazines, TV or radio are all mass-broadcast media where the only hope is to tailor the ad to the centre of some perceived 'segment' of the market. Furthermore, great effort must be made to make the advertisement appealing to the viewer since his or her involvement is limited to watching or listening. The ultimate ad would make the whole experience of advertising interactive, compelling, personalized and addictive.

As digital TV, the Internet and the PC become ubiquitous, so advertising on these media will grow up and realize the true possibilities. Developments in virtual worlds, intelligent agents and evolutionary software can create a whole new kind of ad, which shapes itself to your liking. The simplest idea is that the ad contains intelligent agents that communicate with your agents to determine your likes and dislikes. Thus the TV shows only advertisements that are about products of interest to you, or are presented in a way that appeals to you. Of course, this simplest first step opens whole new avenues to explore about how we pay for services. In effect, advertisements that your agent permits on your TV could fund the cost of your pay-per-view. With the TV becoming, in the future, a home communication and entertainment centre it is very easy to see how, using microphones and cameras (essential attachments for any twenty-first-century interface), the agents can be sure that you are present, and monitor your reaction for feedback. Now at this point choosing to watch an ad can fund your viewing directly.

Virtual-worlds technology opens a further possibility that the ad becomes not something you watch but a world you explore. Why should anyone do this? Because the exploration of the world is enjoyable. Thus the travel industry makes a virtual 'Italy' that is educational, fun and interesting, so people experience Italy and desire the holiday through the experience. The next step is to populate the world with artificial organisms, similar to virtual pets, that are themselves compelling and lead to an emotional bond between viewer and advertiser. Toys such as Tamagotchis, Creatures, Catz and Dogz have already shown that today's simple virtual creatures are tremendously addictive. A world populated by such organisms and then themed by product or by group of companies would make for a deeply emotional interactive experience.

Some of these virtual organisms already breed and evolve, with the users selecting the ones with suitable temperaments. By selectively evolving from those organisms with which the user interacts the most, the advertisement will be populated by the most winsome of the intelligent agents, thus becoming simultaneously personal and deeply compelling. This is the future of advertising because emotion is more important than information.

Such advertisements could be a part of a programme, with the creature watching with you, and as long as you play with it during the broadcast, you get the TV free. If the creature has a relationship with you, similar to that of a pet, you would probably not mind its presence. The advertisement thus becomes a world in which you play, and the messages come to you through sheer enjoyment of that world. The longer you play in the world, the more it shapes itself to match you. It becomes the mechanism to pay for the TV, and may, in its own right, become a viewing experience to justify having a TV. Remember that intelligent agents will destroy brand awareness on Internet shopping, and that a new form of advertising that makes you want to be involved with the brand will be essential.

Agent Society

Individuals clearly do not have the facility to tackle large tasks on their own. They must gather together and organize themselves in some manner to gain mutual advantage. For millennia, this has been the role of societies and organizations. The excess grown by farmers enables a society to use people for non-agrarian tasks, such as appeasing the gods, fighting or developing new tools. The control and distribution of the excess, and the allocation of resources to different tasks, have been the responsibility of those who govern. Hierarchies have developed to manage effectively the filtering of information needed to tackle tasks cooperatively. Those filtering the information have also frequently exploited their position to select and control the flow for their own purposes.

Until recently, developments in machines have replaced only those people who were commanded – manual operators, clerics etc. The complex negotiation skills believed to be necessary for higher management functions were sacrosanct. Organizational structure was driven by the necessity of having skilled negotiators in close proximity. However, improved communications are enabling the negotiators to be distributed around the globe, while still maintaining the fast face-to-face contact needed. But human negotiators are slow, and can cope with problems only up to a certain level of complexity. Once the task exceeds the ability of one or two people to understand all the facets, teams are needed and information must flow and be filtered, regardless of whether this is in a society or in a company. This immediately introduces communication bottlenecks and hierarchies. Furthermore, the organizations set up to deal with these situations are slow to evolve their structures to cope with changing problems. Could we redesign companies in a completely new light using the negotiation skills and information-filtering of intelligent agents? In agent technology, organization and structure are fleeting, transient features that emerge spontaneously from the cooperation process, to be replaced the moment the need arises.

Imagine a world where everyone buys and sells their services and information electronically through the mediation of their own personal agent. You could sell your services to whichever temporary group of people needed to buy your skills at that point in time. It would be possible to negotiate deals to work for a dozen 'companies' all in one day! The wages for a job or the value of a piece of information would be set quickly by need, timeliness and availability. The control of resource allocation and information flow would move from the traditional middlemen who now facilitate the function of our inefficient markets to the negotiating agents. This would have a profound effect on company organization.

The real fundamental change to society is this ability to remove those management functions that have for millennia underpinned our understanding of social structures. Peculiarly, in the scenario we have envisaged above, we will return to something more akin to a hunter-gatherer society, where each day people band together in small groups to obtain resources more efficiently; something, in fact, more suited to the way we have biologically evolved rather than culturally developed. Perhaps the resulting society will be easier to live in – not the terrible, remote and isolated one pictured by many who see information highways as alienating us from each other. And perhaps, too, the use of ourselves as the providers of information, and of our agents as the filters and controllers of the subsequent flow, will change the way our political and social systems function.

Agent Culture

Widespread use of agents in every area of our lives will have a strong impact on our culture. Agents will stand between people and the messages others want to put across. They will kill traditional brand imagery as used in adverts by doing the buying and selling. They will destroy the power of large companies by creating small, dynamic clusters that thrive on a single job then break apart. They will put people in touch with others of shared opinions, reinforcing minority sexual, political or religious mores. It will be easier to find a soul mate elsewhere than in one's own backyard. The very bedrock of nationalism – the closeness of geographic neighbours and the assumption that those far away are unrelated – will be undermined.

The Internet has already begun this process. However, like most things on the current Internet, it is slow and laborious. It takes too long for inexperienced users to find anything, let alone a suitable friend. The real importance of agents is that by searching all day and night, by watching both behaviour and information, and by acting for you, they will bring people in touch more rapidly.

Agent culture is thus one where minorities thrive. Most people form friendships with very small groups of people and strong affiliations with one or two causes. The future, therefore, is a world full of individuals and small groups. The segments so loved by marketing and politics will vanish. People will begin to expect their governments to be like their jobs – transitory and dynamic. A government may hold power long enough only to pass the single law people voted it in for. The sense of culture, of national identity and of personal identity will all change. Agent-driven culture will be a very strange place, where consensus will be impossible to achieve.

II

THE IMPACT ON CREATIVITY

Computer-Enhanced Creativity and Design

For a long time creativity and most artistic pursuits have been held up as something special. We pay a premium to those who can create books, films or music. But, as we explore here, this may be about to change for ever. Many people have in their heads the film they would like to watch or the music they would like to hear. But their ability to generate it prevents them from ever expressing the ideas they have. Recently, video cameras and editing desks have been developed that could enable everyone to become a film-maker. But despite the desire, most people still find it frustrating to turn their ideas into actuality. The tools are insufficient, so we need help in their use.

Recent experiments in pictures, videos and music suggest that a whole new group of tools that will enable people to express themselves are about to emerge. In the past, it has been attempted to emulate the perceived thought processes of experts via rules, and to produce an intelligent helper. The new technique uses one of the great universal mechanisms – evolution. The user is simply presented with a number of pieces of music or art and asked to select which he likes or which is nearest to the desired end. The favourites are recombined with some random changes to produce a whole new set. Slowly, the process converges on a piece of art that is an expression of the user's own mental image. Suddenly, it becomes possible for the computer to tease out from the most incompetent practitioner his own masterpiece. Not that the rest of the world would agree, because this is art, perfected for that specific person at that specific time. Suddenly again, a further opportunity expresses itself. Art can be created by groups, producing output that is a synthesis of their likes and dislikes. A group of teenage girls could create their own music unique to them as a badge of their collective identity. Creative art could once more be a communal expression in just the same way as we believe many of the large Egyptian projects were.

The effect on the creative industries could be immense; after all, the computers have access to a much wider database of material than any living artist, and their technique for manipulating that material is not limited by their own likes or dislikes. As living books and films become common, and computer-assisted creativity takes off, what is the role of the creative middleman? He cannot join the 'caring' professions, and his statements of personal philosophy will be no more interesting than other people's statements. He may continue selling works to a small group of purists, while most people will have their art produced by machines according to their own tastes.

A profound issue will also surround copyright. It is much easier to create your own personal dream by starting somewhere near it. Should I pay for the starting point? If so, how can I identify where the starting point was, if all you see is the end result? Good starting points will have value – how can they be realized? The group-created material is even more worrying from a commercial viewpoint, as each person's contribution will be subsumed into the overall whole. Perhaps the artificial value put on the name of the artist, which prevents copies being worth the same, will vanish, as art will have little financial value at all in the world of computer-assisted recreation.

Computer Creativity

Until very recently, the idea that a computer could be creative was largely ridiculed. Fervent supporters of machine intelligence could see no reason why it should not be, but equally fervent opponents argued that there was something unique about the human brain that prevented machines based on logic from ever being creative.

However, a computer program now exists that re-creates the jazz improvisation of Charlie Parker (one of the greatest improvisers ever) to such an extent that its output could be passed off as 'lost' Parker pieces. The program works by analysing Parker's music and then re-creating similar patterns of notes and combinations. The music created is not a simple imitation of Parker's – it is genuinely new, yet undoubtedly in his style. Most people work by copying and changing styles from others, perfecting and refining them. Very little that is created is totally novel. If the program can perform as well as Parker, then it could do the same for many musicians, enabling the computer to create new music in many styles.

This living music is perhaps the first real challenge to people's deeper acceptance of what computers can do. This is surprising, as the creativity of evolution has been understood for some time. The use of random changes and the recombination of the good bits have been used to explain brain-cell growth, learning and immune systems, and employed to evolve and to create new computer software and hardware. This process bears a great resemblance to many artistic pursuits and may be a universal biological mechanism.

With computers able to access vastly more knowledge than a single person, and with their ability to transform and relate it quickly in many different ways, the exploitation of evolutionary techniques to produce new ideas and art will come quickly. The limitation for computers is that in order to know whether the art generated is acceptable, they must perceive it in a similar manner to humans. Either they need a similar sensory system or, alternatively, human helpers. The latter is 'computer-assisted creativity' and will be here first. But it may be early in the twenty-first century that computers crunching vast databases and applying evolutionary and mutational programs to the data create most of the new ideas. One more aspect of the 'specialness' of being human will then disappear.

Living Books, Films and Music

Bringing a book to life is not about merely animating it. In a living book, the characters are intelligent agents who interact with you and each other. They form a virtual soap opera. Such books could appear soon, since it is already possible to create creatures with moods and behaviours that people anthropomorphize.

Currently, such creatures are not able to converse, creating instead relationships closer to the family pet. However, in denying the emotional appeal and the ability of such systems to create the feeling of life, most neutral observers miss an important human response: the ability to attribute lifelike or human-like characteristics to inanimate or non-human objects. This is done with pets, cars, ships and anything sufficiently complex and continuous in operation that it 'has a life of its own'. Once computer interfaces are built to show lifelike properties, many people will ascribe life to them. Once these interfaces then have natural-language abilities, they will begin to live lives of their own that we can share. A book will cease to be a book. It will become a virtual world that we inhabit as an observer or a participant.

Much of television will be replaced by such synthetic acting. Scriptwriters will create worlds and characters with particular behaviour patterns and then let them build their own story. Such 'second-order' storytelling – one step removed from prescribing the plot by setting up the motivations and leaving the actors to follow it through – will produce a completely new form of story. A living book may have your direct participation, might wander to its conclusion regardless of your 'viewing', or even more bizarrely might use your emotional response to drive where the story goes.

Living music is much the same. It uses your interaction with it to change the music that is being played, following your mood up or down, changing with your expression and degree of interest. Music would cease to be a thing that you listened to repeatedly but would become more like a walk in the garden – something that subtly changed in response to your emotions.

Technology currently limits us so that what we get from films, music or books is fixed and repeated. Indeed, we assume for some reason that this is how it should be. Actually, the rest of our life is full of unrepeatable events, both large and small, and both in and out of our control. The human brain evolved to survive in such a world; it is stimulated by change and it screens out repetition. Living art forms will finally use technology to bring art to the point where the brain can fully participate in it. Furthermore, by living with and through the art, we will become more than passive viewers. We, too, will become creators. Living films, books and music will enable us to live our best stories ever.

Living Games

A modern computer game is a very difficult and demanding thing to write successfully. It must have stunning graphics, appealing game play and often a computer opponent of just the right difficulty level. To be a big seller it must achieve all of these things and cater for a wide variety of users, all of whom have different perceptions about what makes a good game, good graphics, etc., and all of whom have different abilities at playing it. No wonder games designers find it hard to get a big hit, and when one does, the rest quickly mimic it.

Obviously, most computer opponents are computers. The rise of network games, where people can play more challenging opponents (or those whose play patterns are less predictable, even when they are easier), is directly attributable to the difficulty and lack of power in today's AI systems. The development of artificial life forms, virtual worlds and intelligent agents, however, could lead to a new kind of computer game, one that is shaped by the very play pattern that the user creates himself. This can occur at two levels. Firstly, the computer can create more elements of the type the user plays with the most, using the time spent on the game to drive the mechanisms described elsewhere for creating art and music to shape the structural elements of the game. Secondly, the creatures populating the world can use artificial-life techniques to evolve – clearly the ones the user does not like or can beat get 'removed', whereas the ones he rewards survive and flourish. With care, this leads to a game where the opponents are always just a fraction more difficult than you, and where you build up a collection of favourite friends to help you.

As the artificial-life techniques and the behaviours of these creatures move from lifelike to human-like, we slowly get to the point where, in the game environment, it is difficult to tell people's reactions from those of machines. This could result from the process of selecting more-natural behaviours among their creatures, or by the invention of better artificial-life techniques.

Such games become self-configuring. The elements present are those that are most attractive to the user, not to the designer. This requires a different mentality, very challenging to today's creators. Many producers and directors make the games they want to play or think the market will like. These new games of the future will be tool kits, shaped by the play pattern to become the user's own game; this is a tough concept for focus-group fans or marketeers to grasp. Indeed, the radical change in the way 'living products' should be thought about is going to cause pain among many who value their skills in the market-place. We are moving from first-order markets (I sell what I think you like) to second-order markets (I sell what enables you to create what you like). Games could be one of the leaders in creating this new way of thinking.

Such market-places have a unique danger, though. The ultimate computer game would be a 'Total Addiction' – a game that shapes itself to the elements you most like to play in such a manner that it totally satisfies you. You never want to stop playing. However, any self-configuring activity in which your pleasure is used to shape that activity always has such risks inherent in it. Will we see one day the government insisting that games have time limiters the way that some motor vehicles have speed limiters?

III

THE IMPACT ON FINANCIAL SYSTEMS

Money

Already, people are buying things across the Internet. Mostly, they hand over a credit-card number, but some transactions already use electronic cash. The transactions are secure, so the cash does not go astray or disappear; nor can it be forged easily. Using such cash will eventually become an everyday occurrence for us all.

Electronic cash based on smart cards has already been found to work well. The smart cards allow owners to 'load' small amounts of money for use in transactions where small change would normally be used: paying bus fares, buying sweets, etc. The cards are equivalent to a purse. But they can and will allow much more. Of course, electronic cash does not have to be held on a card. It can equally well be 'stored' in the network. Such transactions require secure messaging across the system. Currently, the cost of this messaging makes it uneconomic for small transactions. But in due course the network-based option will become more attractive, especially as you no longer lose money when you lose the card.

When cash is digitized, it loses some of the restrictions of physical cash. Imagine that a child has a cash card. Her parents can give her pocket money, dinner money, clothing allowance and so on. They can all be labelled separately, so that she cannot spend all her dinner money on chocolate (electronic shopping can, of course, provide the information needed to enable the cash). She may also have restrictions about how much of her pocket money she may spend on various items. There is no reason why children could not implement their own economies, swapping tokens and IOUs. Of course, in the adult world these grow up into local exchange trading systems (LETS), where people exchange tokens – a glorified babysitting circle. But these LETSs do not have to be just local: wider circles could be set up, even globally, to allow people to exchange services or information with each other.

Electronic cash can be versatile enough to allow for negotiable cash. Credit may be exchanged as cash, and cash could be labelled with source. For instance, we may see 'celebrity cash' signed by a well-known person, worth more because they have used it. Cash may be labelled as tax paid, so those donations from cards to charities could automatically expand with the recovered tax. Alternatively, any sales tax could be recovered at the point of sale. With these advanced facilities, it becomes obvious that the cash needs to become better woven into taxation, auditing and accounting systems. These functions can be much more streamlined as a result, with less human administration. When ID verification is added to the transactions, we can guarantee who is carrying them out. We can then implement personal taxation, with people paying different amounts for the same goods. This would work only for certain types of purchase – for physical goods there would otherwise be a thriving black market.

But one of the best advantages of making cash digital is the seamlessness of international purchases. Even without common official currency, the electronic cash systems would become *de facto* international standards, reducing the currency-exchange charges we currently pay to the banks every time we change money. This is one of the justifications often cited for European monetary union, but it is happening anyway in global e-commerce.

Decline of Capitalism
It is often assumed that automation would improve a country's gross domestic product (GDP); that is, that it would increase national income, since firms employing it would become more profitable and their former workers would go off and find other work. Automation is financially desirable for a firm simply if the increase in its income is greater than its increase in costs. However, a country gains as a whole only if the net cost of providing redundant workers with either new work or benefits equivalent to their previous remuneration is

less than the saving or profit rise from automation. It is important to note that the overall cost of maintaining the society in its previous style would increase, since the income must now pay for both the people and the machines. Hopefully, though, this cost increase would be less than the increase in overall wealth generation. However, fewer people would be actively involved in generating this wealth. If automation is carried out sensibly, with due regard to national and global consequences, then a leisure society could eventually result. People may work purely voluntarily, perhaps for different goals than financial benefit; or they could devote more energy to pursuits that improve the quality of their lives.

But in traditional capitalist socio-economic systems, companies may employ automation without regard to the cost to the whole population. Similarly, countries may make use of automation to improve their international competitiveness, sometimes at the expense of other countries. As automation becomes more widespread, there may be, increasingly, an overall (global) cost greater than the local saving in each case, since there may not be sufficient profitable work to provide replacement income for those people losing their jobs.

The traditional capitalist system has worked very well to increase local, national and global wealth for many years. However, for the reasons above, it may have peaked already, and, if not, it may do so soon. If pure capitalism is pursued after the peak, damage will undoubtedly result, since local gains will be more than offset by global loss. If this were to continue indefinitely, the ultimate result would be not a situation where a very few people owned all the wealth (which is often assumed would be the case), but the grinding to a halt of the entire economy. Otherwise, either there would be no one who could afford the output of the remaining companies, or corporate taxation would need to be so high to support the population in an acceptable style that the companies would make unsatisfactory profits and fizzle out. Either way spells doom. Clearly, pure capitalism without regard to the external consequence of internal automation cannot be self-sustaining for much longer. The only uncertainty is when a new system need be introduced.

Stock Market

The stock exchange long since stopped being a trading floor with scraps of paper and became a distributed computer environment – it effectively moved into cyberspace. The deals still take place, but in cyberspace. There are no virtual environments yet, but the other tools, such as automated buying and selling, already exist. These computers are becoming smarter, and exist in cyberspace in every way that people do. As a result, there is more automated analysis, easier visualization and more computer-assisted dealing. People will be able to see which shares are doing well, to spot trends and to act on their computer's advice at a push of a button.

However, as we see more people buying personal access to share-dealing software to determine best buys, or even to automatically buy or sell on certain clues, we will see some very negative behaviour. Firstly, traffic will be highly correlated if personal computers can all act on the same information at the same time. We will see information waves, and also enormous swings in share prices. Most private individuals will suffer because of this, while institutions and people with better software will benefit. This is because prices will rise and fall simply because of the correlated activity of automated AI software and not because of any real effects related to the shares themselves. Institutions may have to limit private share transactions to control the problem; but they could also make a lot of money from modelling the software themselves and thus determining in advance what the recommendations and actions will be, capitalizing enormously on the resultant share movements, and indeed even stimulating them. Of course, if the share-dealing public perceives this problem, the AI software will not sell well, so the problem will not arise. High-volume sales need public trust. What is more likely is that such software will sell in limited quantities, causing the effects to be significant, but not destroying the markets.

A money-making scam is therefore highly possible. A company need only write some reasonably good share-portfolio-management software for it to capture a fraction of the available market. The company writing the software will, of course, understand how it works and what the effects of a piece of information will be (which they will ensure they receive at the same time), and thus would be able to predict the buying or selling activity of the subscribers. If they were then to produce another service which makes recommendations, they would have even more notice of an effect and would be able to influence prices directly. They would then be in the position of the top market forecasters who know their advice will be self-fulfilling. This is neither insider dealing nor fraud, and, once the software captures a significant share, the quality of its advice would be very high, decoupling share performance from the real world. Only the last people to react would lose out, paying the most, or selling at the lowest price, as the price is restored to a 'correct' level by the stock exchange – and, of course, even this is predictable to a point. The fastest will profit the most.

The most significant factor is the proportion of share dealing influenced by that company's software. The problem is that software markets tend to be dominated by just two or three companies, and the nature of this type of software is that there is strong positive reinforcement for the company with the biggest influence, and this could quickly lead to a virtual monopoly. Moreover, it does not really matter whether the software is based on visualization tools or AI: each can have predictability associated with it.

It is interesting to contemplate the effects this widespread automated dealing would have on the stock market. Crashes due to unrestricted automated dealing are unlikely to happen again, but it certainly looks as if prices will occasionally become decoupled from actual value, and price swings will become more significant. Of course, much money can be made from predicting the swings or getting access to the software-critical information before someone else does, so we may see a need for equalized delivery services. Without equalized delivery, those closest to the dealing point would be able to buy or sell first, and since the swings could be extremely rapid, this would be very important. Dealers would have to have price information immediately, and of course the finite speed of light does not permit this. If dealing time is quantified, that is, if share prices are updated at fixed intervals, the duration of the interval becomes all important, and will strongly affect the nature of the market, for instance, whether everyone in that interval pays the same or the first to take action gains the advantage.

Also of interest is the possibility of agents acting on behalf of many people to negotiate among themselves to increase the price of a company's shares, and then to sell at a pre-negotiated time or signal. Such automated systems would also be potentially vulnerable to false information from people or agents hoping to capitalize on their correlated behaviour.

In addition, there are potential legal problems. Suppose I were to write, and sell to a company, a piece of AI-based share-dealing software which learns by itself how stock-market fluctuations arise. Suppose it later commits a fraud such as insider dealing (I might not have explained the law, or the law may have changed since I wrote the software). Who would then be liable?

The Leisure Society and the Black-Box Economy

The black-box economy is a strictly theoretical possibility, but it could result in a situation where machines gradually take over more and more roles until the whole economy is run by them, with everything automated. People could be gradually displaced by intelligent systems, robots and automated machinery. If this were to proceed to the ultimate conclusion, we could have a system with the same or even greater output as the original society, but with no people involved. The manufacturing process could thus become a 'black box'. Such a system would be so controlled by machines that humans would not easily be able to pick up the pieces if it crashed – they would simply not understand how it works, nor would they be able to control it. It would be a fly-by-wire economy.

The human effort could be reduced to simple requests. When you want a new television, a robot might come and collect the old set, recycling the materials and bringing you a new one. Since no people need be involved, and since the whole automated system could be entirely self-maintaining and self-sufficient, there could be no costs at all. This concept may be equally applicable in other sectors, such as services and information – ultimately producing more leisure time.

Although such a system is theoretically possible – energy is free in principle, and resources are ultimately a function of energy availability – it is unlikely to go quite this far. Nevertheless, there will always be some jobs that we do not want to automate, so some people may still work, but much of this work may be voluntary. This could be the leisure economy we were promised long ago. Just because futurists predicted it in the past and it has not happened yet does not mean that it never will.

IV

THE IMPACT ON PHYSICAL THINGS

The Future of Television
Television is one of the great success stories of the twentieth century. It took decades before it was clear what people wanted from it, as it gradually became less of a formal platform and more of an entertainment medium. Current technology limits affordable screen area to typically one per cent of the field of view, and to only audio-visual stimulation. We are quite some way from the holodeck with totally convincing full sensory immersion. However, flat screens will soon hang on our living-room walls. A 1.5-metre (54-inch) diagonal plasma screen for less that £2,000 should be available by 2001. This is still outside the budget of most homes, which will have screens less than a metre (36 inches) across for some time. Visual immersion is unlikely, apart from goggles, until after 2020, by which time we will hopefully be able to afford a small room with fully polymer-screen-lined walls and maybe three-dimensional capacity, with the appropriate bandwidth to drive these with acceptable resolution. In this room, we will be able to escape into our fantasy world.

Polymer screens may eventually win out, but the battle will be fought in various niches between a wide range of screen techno-logies, plasma and bonded LCD panels being the two strongest current contenders. Screens that are primarily TVs will have many other uses, especially if they hang on walls. They can act as virtual fish tanks, displays for electronic paintings downloaded from galleries around the world, virtual windows showing real-time views out on to a Bahamas beach, or life-size video-communication panels to allow people to share a cup of coffee across the oceans.

But whatever the display technology, digital TV will soon be the norm. On the back of digitization, television will be made far more

interesting by interactivity, indexing, choice of view, associated information, and video capture and manipulation. But the biggest
advantage of making TV digital in the long term will be its
integration into the computer world. The arguments over whether
computers will be integrated into TVs or vice versa are mostly over.
Both have happened as costs have fallen.

What is less clear is what will happen next. With digital TV set-
top boxes having high computing capability, providing Internet
access, games, e-mail, home shopping and information, what is the
incentive for a home without a conventional computer to buy one?
By contrast, homes with computers and TVs with their sophisticated
set-top boxes may still use their computers for the more computery
things and their TVs for watching programmes. There may be a
strong cultural split in the market.

Indeed, it is likely that the Internet and TV will simply converge,
eventually, with TV being just another Internet service, with all the
search facilities, indexing, chat forums and, most importantly, worldwide access to any channel (obviously subject to local laws, subscrip-
tions, etc.). This will open up the global TV market while giving
people what they want rather than just what happens to be shown on
a few local channels. Computer agents will be able to organize passive viewing to our taste, acting as assemblers for virtual channels.
The agent may appear to the viewer as a friendly face with a friendly
personality behind it, which may also have responsibility for non-TV
tasks, too, such as shopping around. With sufficient intelligence, the
agent itself may become part of the entertainment, playing live
music that it writes in real time, or taking us on a guided teletravel
expedition. With adequate indexing, it will one day be possible for
agents to assemble customized programmes on a particular theme
that may not have previously existed.

With an infinite number of potential channels, it will be possible
to sit and watch traffic jams in your local town, or remotely attend a
council meeting, as well as watch any one of the many coffee
percolators on the Internet (one of the earliest use of web-cams was
to see if there was any coffee left in the percolator). Remotely

accessing video cameras has many trivial uses, but also permits more-useful activities such as allowing parents to check on their children at playgroup. Certainly, community TV is likely to grow.

Surprisingly, perhaps, computer games are rapidly becoming a spectator activity just like sport, and we may see all the same trappings becoming associated with them, such as premier leagues. Watching other everyday activities has already proved to be successful TV viewing in the many real-life docusoaps, and these will evolve easily into the Internet and digital TV.

However, what these mostly point to is that people are content. When we have catered for our basic survival needs, socializing is the next most important human activity, and is the primary driver for many platforms. The Internet was originally constructed to allow sharing of scientific information. When it matures, we will find that most of the human use is for socializing. Whether machines talking to machines will dominate even this remains to be seen.

MUST USE

The Future of the Phone Box

Phone boxes have changed dramatically in the past decades, but they are still basically a phone in a box. In the future, we can expect rather more change. The phone box itself may be simply the centre of a wider zone in which it will offer high-speed wireless communication services. It may offer several zones in fact, providing access to mobile networks from far away. It will be able, therefore, to act as a centre for low-speed services, to provide coordinates and navigation information, perhaps to allow electronic cash exchange, even to offer low-speed radio LAN capability. Closer in, passive picocell (a very-high-bandwidth but short-range radio system) technology will allow it to offer services at much higher data rates up to 100Mbit/s. This will enable people to send or receive large files and software, to synchronize their computers, or to access Internet services at high speed. Just walking within a hundred metres (300 feet) of a phone box may be sufficient to ensure that e-mail transactions are carried out. This will give a valuable halfway point between full mobility and the fixed network. The high bandwidth of the fixed network will be accessible from a large zone near any phone box, enabling fixed and mobile networks to converge.

In the box itself, infrared communications may offer still higher rates, though it is hard to see what might require higher rates than can be delivered over passive picocell. The box may seem fairly empty. Most functionality could be provided by vandal-resistant voice or visual interfaces, with no need for any slots that might be vulnerable to the insertion of foreign objects. Cash could be replaced either by smart cards or by iris-scan identification. An anti-noise environment would allow loud-speaking telephones to be used without the problems of traffic drowning out the conversation, while ensuring privacy. With no handset to cut off, nothing obvious to break, and no cash to steal, there would be less attraction for vandals. With built-in video surveillance, even graffiti would be deterred.

If the box can be made more secure by using such technologies as video surveillance and iris-scan identification, then perhaps video services could be incorporated in most places. With display technology plummeting in cost, even a holodeck environment would not be impossible. The floor of the box could actually be the top of a rolling ball that tracks the movement of the occupant while allowing him to walk as far as he likes in any direction, immersed in a fully three-dimensional virtual environment. With virtual meetings, video-conferencing, or pure fantasy teletravel, using the phone might be the least of the services these boxes would be used for.

The video display could offer talking-head-style interfaces, adjusted automatically for the language of the occupant, perhaps even for their culture. Voice and gesture recognition and natural language-processing, including translation, should be adequately developed in about ten years. The advanced audio-visual interface will allow the emulation of virtual machines, so the box could essentially replicate any sort of terminal. With the inclusion of some means of providing high-quality hard prints, the boxes could offer ticketing, photograph printing, and many other services. Scanning technology would enhance their capability even further, allowing transfer of physical pictures. Of course, electronic cash management, information or software purchases, or electronic shopping could all be feasible in such a box. Or people might 'fill up' a portable entertainment device before proceeding on their journey.

It is expected that in the future people will carry a wide range of electronic devices on their person, in other words 'wearables'. Some of these may communicate with each other via the skin, which offers a high-capacity medium, but perhaps some will need a more conventional interface. This could be offered in the phone box, which could create a nano-LAN to link together and interpret protocols between the machines as required. Although unfeasible with current technologies, it may be possible in future to recharge batteries almost instantly, and this could be another useful potential service offered in the box.

Finally, the screens in the boxes may be used for advertising purposes, and this could offset some of the cost of the calls being made. It may even be possible to have video advertisements on the boxes' exterior. More environmentally pleasing, the same facility would allow the boxes to be camouflaged so that they blended in well with the local environment. Soon they may be virtually invisible except for a discreet beacon.

Future Buildings

Housing will change slowly, lagging far behind technology capability. New homes today still come with just five or six electrical sockets in the living room, though there may be many more devices needing power. The building industry seems very slow to react to the demands of new technology. Existing houses will stand for many years, so we will have to make do or adapt.

Prefabricated buildings are expected by architectural futurists to make a strong comeback in the United States, and possibly in Europe, too. Prefabricated modules can be assembled to make a wide variety of designs, making high-specification homes at a much lower cost. It is simply easier to make the complex structures required in factories than on a building site. These modules may make good use of smart materials. Panels may change their thermal properties and even rigidity according to the weather, and may have sensors built in to monitor structural stress and strain. These materials may be more windproof, and even more resistant to earthquakes. We may see anti-noise technology built into the panels to provide a quieter interior. Some panels may incorporate solar cells. Window panels may use holographic embossing to deflect sunlight to the whole room. Others may have panels that can switch electronically between windows and screens. Colour-change materials may be used externally for thermal adjustment, and internally to react to the mood of the inhabitants. Such effects could eventually be linked into digital TV, or be used to create the right atmosphere for a party. Electronic wallpaper need not be fixed in pattern or colour but may be variable, though this would be more expensive. Far in the future, this wallpaper may evolve into fully functional displays that can be used to make a dining room into a medieval banquet hall for the evening, or to take part in a virtual conference. People could teletravel using a large screen in their living room or maybe from a small box room with fully lined walls, ceiling and floor.

One important feature that will eventually be needed is the home network, linking appliances together and providing an interface to the outside world. This could be based on existing electrical wiring or could be wireless, using radio or infrared technology. Appliances in the near future will have a great deal of communications and computing capability, and they will need access to such networks to do their job effectively. For instance, a future washing machine might interrogate chips in the clothes, read the identifiers in the washing powder, then decide on a suitable wash by talking to the various manufacturers' computers. It would then switch itself on at a time when the electricity company has agreed it will get the cheapest rate. Similarly, a domestic iris-scan unit could end the trauma of losing a set of house keys. Or, when the occupier is away from the house, a video intercom would allow him or her to meet a workman at the front door, let him in and monitor the job. Chips-with-everything. Domestic robots will also make good use of the home network to stay in touch with each other.

We will also need networks in the home for data and video distribution. It is unlikely that there will be only one home computer, and yet all may need access to the same data, and may want to feed images to any display. Perhaps a single digital TV decoder could feed all the TVs, video recorders, electronic paintings and shopping tablets in the home instead of having to be replicated many times.

There will be many displays: some hanging on walls, some standing on work surfaces, and others lying flat on tables. A future with just one screen for all functions would result in rapid family breakdown. Personal displays will become essential for domestic harmony. Some may be magazine-sized tablets; others might use goggles and headphones. The developing audio technology to position a sound in three-dimensional space will become very useful.

If we get it right, displays will be about the only visible evidence of high technology. There will soon be no need for all the black products we see today. The hi-fi, computing and TV stacks will vanish, replaced by integrated boxes of tricks under the stairs that have audio and video links with every room. Speakers can be flat and hidden in walls or even in the screens, so that sounds come from the same place as the visual source.

Public buildings will change in many of the same structural and cosmetic ways. We can expect bigger screens, and it will be more economically feasible to justify high-capability entertainment zones. Voice interfaces may often be less appropriate because of crowd noise, and, in any case, for control purposes only a few people would be authorized to use them. Tall buildings will make more use of smart and reactive materials than will homes, and it may also be more feasible to include the latest weather-responsive and energy-efficient mechanisms. Security robots may be much more commonplace, looking for fires and intruders, and there will be more video surveillance. In short, we will see many of the same changes as in the home, but probably rather earlier. Public buildings may work well with new forms of transportation, allowing people to travel to and fro in relative ease, and popular locations would make ideal sites for transport nodes.

One of the most important changes we will see with many public buildings is their networking. Obviously they will have LANs, but additionally they will have extensive links to the outside world, allowing people to visit from afar, and perhaps permitting people in the building to see and communicate with some of these visitors. There could be extensive links with other public buildings, which may be represented by virtual buildings. It will be possible to add a virtual gallery or two by using large screens, which could show works actually on display in a distant gallery. Friendly faces on screens may be those of artificial intelligences replacing people. Even the bank's cash machine may get a face, or many, depending on the customer. Social zones, such as coffee bars, cafés and pubs, could include virtual meeting places where distant friends may be included in the socializing with those physically present. Such cyber-socializing could be very dependent on fashion: the difference between 'sad' and 'cool' is not technological. Investments in such areas must, therefore, be risky at best. Meeting new friends electronically may be equally possible, using smart badges or Internet agents, but its market success is surely even more dependent on fashion.

Cuddly Robots and Virtual Friends

The cuddly pet robot is about to burst on to the stage. As cute as any pet, less mess and bother, and able to attune perfectly to your desires, the cuddly robot will be the first major use of artificial intelligence in the home. Until very recently, artificial intelligence was concerned with the lofty goal of emulating human intelligence – a worthy but largely unsuccessful goal so far. More recently, however, the field of artificial life has concentrated on producing lifelike behaviours. Untroubled by the need for logic or natural language it has shown that it is much easier to produce an adaptive, animal-like system. The success of simple toys such as Tamagotchis showed that this level of emulation is sufficient. People want living computers and robots. In the living interface section we discussed how tone recognition opens emotional channels. A cuddly robot simply needs to respond to voice tone, show adaptive behaviour and look 'right'.

The development of better miniature actuators and smart materials will make such robots affordable for all. Indeed, with the rise of animal welfare concerns and health issues the idea of imprisoning a pet in your house may become totally unacceptable and the only civilized pet will be a robot.

Of course, as the pet's natural-language abilities increase, it will become increasingly common to converse with your cuddly robot, which in turn will act as your mentor, guide and confidant. Psychologically programmed robots will also become common. The cuddly robot may be a major route through which we communicate with the world of information. It will be the first step to a virtual friend.

Even today, people's feeling of alienation causes much surprising behaviour. The high use of telephone chat groups among perfect strangers, and friendships on the worldwide web between people who have never met, both attest to the desire to find mind friends. Multi-player dungeons contain not only people but also bots – non-human programs that imitate people. Some are sufficiently realistic that young males try to chat up the female personas they represent. A sad behaviour possibly, but perhaps a pointer to a common twenty-first-century occurrence. Much of the time we do not want great intelligence in our friends, just empathy, some bland advice and listening skills. We can be certain that this is a combination that computers will easily deliver. The growth of virtual friends will match that of cuddly pets.

V

The Impact on Social Institutions and Behaviour

Telework Centres

Much of this book has been written on trains between London and Ipswich, using a Psion Series 5 palmtop computer. With a cellphone adaptor, the same computer can be connected to the Internet and, hence, to any other networked computer in the world. It really is possible to work from almost anywhere. This has led to predictions that many people will work from home, perhaps up to 20–25 per cent of the population. However, it is common for teleworkers to continue to work a few days each week in a conventional office. People still want to have the social contact that work offers, and want to stay in regular touch with their co-workers. Another, rarely mentioned problem with teleworking is that many people who work from home do not really have enough space. Not everyone lives in a large house with a comfortable office. People may squash a desk into a corner of a living room; it is not unheard of to use even the bathroom. As work becomes increasingly suitable for teleworking, many more people will want to do so and their firms may encourage it. So what do we do?

One solution we expect to see is the conversion of redundant buildings into local telework centres, where people could go to work alongside their neighbours, but for different companies. The buildings would be equipped with adequate networking and facilities, and could have a mixture of hot desks for infrequent occupants and permanently allocated desks for regular users. Single companies with a significant local presence may permanently lease some desks. Obviously, the buildings could have open-plan areas or offices, or both. Sharing of space and equipment could make such centres cost-effective, especially if some of the users were shift or night workers.

Using state-of-the art cordless LANs and cordless phones, equipment and desks could be moved around frequently without the usual problems of rearranging spaghetti wiring.

In this way, space problems at home are avoided, and people still get social contact at work so they do not feel so isolated. But there are other more hidden benefits. Firstly, people will have more-frequent contact with many more of their neighbours. We think this will have a positive effect on local communities. Secondly, there is more scope for cross-fertilization and education, making a better-educated and more versatile workforce. Thirdly, people would be able to change employers without having to move geographically. This would gradually make it is easier to set up and run virtual companies, where companies could form teams of dispersed people with just the right skills for a particular project, who would go their separate ways when the project had terminated.

Another possible community benefit of the centres would be that they could also be used out of office hours for other activities, such as night school. Large screens that allow life-size video-conferencing, photocopying and printing equipment, meeting rooms and of course computer terminals could be just as useful for community activities as for work. With immersive virtual-reality chambers, too, the tele-work buildings would be very attractive entertainment centres, perhaps greatly enhancing the quality of life in rural areas. They could also be ideal locations for bureau services, or just for companies to hire for courses or away-days. Hotels have provided basic rooms for such activities for many years, but are yet to realize the need for well-provisioned IT equipment.

These telework centres may also make ideal drop-off places for increasingly frequent teleshopping deliveries. All in all, we can expect that these centres will become very commonplace over the coming years, an ideal investment for budding property speculators.

Towards the Care Economy

Increasing automation will gradually make people more productive, reducing the manpower required, and making some people redundant. In the short term, this is tolerable since new jobs are being created by the new industries and services that are springing up from the shift towards an information economy. However, as machine intelligence gradually increases, and applications and services become more sophisticated, increasing numbers of knowledge workers and other information workers will also lose their jobs. Agencies and middlemen first; information-gatherers, analysts and value-adders later. Finally, information-creators will also suffer from substitution. Many of the professions throughout these levels are vulnerable to wholesale substitution by machine intelligence. Thus, jobs which require knowledge, creativity, decision-making or other intellectual skills, or almost any manufacturing or manual job, are liable to disappear.

Only occupations where people are an essential component of the service, such as caring and personal services, are really safe (even here, some parts of the job which are intellectual are open to substitution). Many of the new jobs being created now or in the near future are transient. Counselling, raising children, nursing, waiting in restaurants, hairdressing, etc. are good examples of jobs where substitution is unlikely for the foreseeable future, while some low-paid work may be uneconomic to automate.

The obvious result of this long-term trend is a shift of value in jobs away from knowledge or skill, towards caring roles where workers are valued because they are people, and their output is basically human interaction. The differentiators are then personality, warmth, etc., rather than efficiency. We may call this the 'care economy'. It is interesting that today many such jobs are valued much less than the intellectual professions. Nevertheless, intellect seems easier for computers to learn than supposedly more simple human interaction skills.

It is also interesting that this economy will have very different demographic characteristics from our present system. While there is currently a premium on the energy, fast thinking and creativity associated with youth, the skills that may become most valued are those that we tend to think of as wisdom, life experience and basic human warmth. In the new economy, older people will find that they are no longer at a disadvantage.

Cyberspace Real Estate – Information, Sales and Meeting Areas

In the 'space' sense of cyberspace, we see an analogy with real estate, and it can be used and marketed in the same ways as physical real estate. There are good positions, centres of traffic, which are thus of high value and can command high premiums. Currently, there are several different kinds.

The first, the likes of Yahoo and the other directory sites, are good examples of highly populated information centres. They act as access points to vast pools of information – business, social, household and personal, including news, magazines, entertainment and links to other areas of the web. They can offer advertising opportunities, and as the sites become more intelligent, they will be able to target the advertising to each individual browser. These sites are similar in concept to libraries. 'Push technology', another competing, but currently declining, Internet technology, is almost the equivalent of newspapers, albeit with some sections thrown away, but still with a hefty amount of advertising. As these evolve, they will become more like themed TV channels, with the user free to set up a tuner for the favourite channels. Music and TV might even be included in their material. Some writers have suggested that this will replace browsing, but they miss the point by a mile. Newsgathering is not the only thing people want from the web, nor even the main thing.

The second kind of traffic centre are the virtual malls. With several shops that people like grouped together in a single site, the virtual mall is similar to a real shopping mall. Many people visit these areas, and those sites with the most attractive position on the screen or the most eye-catching logo will attract business. They make sales and pay large fees to the mall owner, just as in the physical world. The mall owner has to market the mall to make it attract customers, or the shops will not bother with it. The malls may also carry advertising.

The third kind of traffic centre are the meeting areas where people socialize, such as chat rooms. These are multi-user domains, and may use any kind of media for people to communicate with each other. Here the service is simply meeting and interacting, so these sites attract people through the most basic human needs. They can make money by charging for access, or from sales or advertising. People are just another form of attractive content. Users will be attracted to the sites that bring together other people with whom they would want to interact.

These various sites are normally quite distinct from each other, though we are just seeing the next phase, where some sites offer a blend of these activities, growing from being simply a library, mall or meeting area to being a collection of these – a virtual town centre. As this phase develops, we already envisage entire virtual cities offering a wide range of facilities. We will see high hit-rates, and high charges to companies that wish to set up shops there.

PAY TO WHOM.

Future of the City – Geographic

TOWN VERSUS CYBERSPACE

Conventional wisdom has it that cyberspace will never catch on. People will not shop on the net because they like going to 'real shops'. We disagree. Cyberspace offers convenience and efficiency coupled with low prices and total choice. The city offers stress, inefficiency, high prices, limited choice, and having to carry heavy or bulky goods back home on packed, infrequent buses and trains, or, if travelling by car, through heavy traffic. We think that many people will pick convenience, and consequently cyberspace shopping will flourish. There is a similar argument concerning leisure activities, the theatre, for instance. When digital and Internet TV take off, we will not be limited to one play at one theatre in our local town, but will be able to read reviews of any play anywhere and watch it virtually, without having to crane behind the big hat or hairstyle in front to get a good view of the stage. Going into the city is already an infrequent occurrence for millions of people. It will become even more infrequent in the future unless public transport is improved greatly. Most people would be very happy indeed to use public transport if we got it right. So what do we need?

Future bus service

We need frequent buses, with less distance from home to bus stops. To reduce journey time, we need more-direct routes and either very punctual arrivals or an easy way to find out when the next bus will arrive. Satellite positioning systems are already used to provide the latter service, although you still need to go to the bus stop to find out when the bus is coming, unless you have instant Internet access. We also need an efficient and reliable distribution service to deliver our shopping when it is inconvenient to carry it home.

Bus-route planners could learn a lot from telecommunications networks. Star architectures are fine for main routes, but really not much use for linking town centres to individual homes; hence, we have bus stops that may be several minutes walk away, and meandering routes to cover every street in an area. We could solve this problem with local access rings. A bus or minibus would go round in circles all day carrying people between stops close to their homes and a single main-route station for the rest of the journey. This local bus could eventually be unmanned. It could pick up people from their home on request via a simple phone call or Internet communication, helping the old and the frail, or just preventing people from getting wet when it's raining.

The bus from the station to the destination would stop at only a few other major stations, instead of at every street lamp. The local access ring service would effectively remove the need for the 'park' in the park-and-ride schemes for many people, while greatly reducing the number of stops on the route, thus speeding up the service. It would also mean buses that connect much closer to home. With the vast improvement in convenience and journey time, far more people would use the service, which would improve bus companies' profits, while reducing car pollution and congestion and generally improving the local environment. People would be able to have a drink at the theatre without worrying about driving home.

They would not have to worry about their car being vandalized or stolen from a car park. There would be much less traffic and congestion, making it easier to drive in when necessary. Many people would be able to survive completely without cars. Everyone wins. We may still not go into town very often, but at least when we do, it would be a much more pleasant trip.

DISTRIBUTION

The distribution part of the solution will happen anyway. As people shop more from home, there will be a rapidly growing distribution infrastructure, with several deliveries to homes each day. Even if people normally shop in towns, they will often buy through the network simply because it offers more choice and lower prices. Also, we will see many shops in cities receive substantial income from manufacturers for acting as sophisticated try-on outlets. They will offer new services such as laser body-scanning, and will allow people to shop around electronically and to order direct from the manu- facturer, who will produce the clothes to the customer's exact measurements. The retailer will have to adapt or die. The delivery companies will rely on a high level of trust and knowledge of the customer. They will know when someone is at home and will be able to arrange appropriate collection, storage and delivery for any product. They may also deliver to people at their work. Such a delivery system would operate very well with the new telework centres that we expect to appear in the future.

SECURITY AND SURVEILLANCE

Security in cities is improving as more and more video surveillance is being used. Some people complain that this is because crime simply moves elsewhere, but as video networks spread to cover most towns and cities, we can expect overall crime to fall. The same networks allow better traffic control and monitoring of crowds. Local authorities will have much more information about what works and what does not, and will be able to adjust their planning accordingly. Of course, a price is paid in loss of privacy, but so far at least, this is generally accepted. When improved video cameras are linked to much smarter computers that can recognize everyone's face and effectively catalogue everyone's movements, associations and activities, there may be more objections. When this information is additionally linked into all the other databases, government or commerce can assemble a complete picture of our lives. This will be much less acceptable. Finally, given that this information can be stored for ever, there is a danger that it could be used in the future by a malevolent authority.

24-HOUR CITY

In the information economy, more work is information based and can be more easily networked. With better networks and lower global telecommunication prices, it is easy and cheap to work from anywhere. However, the world is not flat and we have time zones. If a job requires contacting people elsewhere in the world, a time shift from the traditional 9am-to-5pm working day is often needed. Many people in cities are now working at any hour, in addition to traditional night workers. The increasing number of global travellers further increases this resident night-working population. The city truly doesn't sleep any more. As the number of night workers increases, so other services such as restaurants will stay open, too. While daytime may still be a peak time, activities will go on right around the clock.

VIRTUAL CITY

Future cities will exist not only as physical places, but will also have a digital presence in cyberspace. The various businesses, social institutions and tourist attractions will be accessible via the network. Plays and concerts may be relayed on to the network and extra 'attendance' fees collected. Local commerce will gain by making their services and goods available to a wider electronic market. The cyberspace overlay on the city may generate large numbers of visits and possibly substantial revenue. Unfortunately, the owners of attractions in many cities are unaware of their future value, and sometimes sell rights to electronic access for a fraction of their eventual worth.

Education in the Information Age

There is a lot of current emphasis on teaching computing in schools, preparing children for the ubiquitous computers they will encounter when they enter the workforce. They are taught to use word-processors and spreadsheets. However, much of this education is based on the false assumption that computing will be basically the same when they leave school. The fact is that most of this teaching is wasted, since computing will be very different in a few years, just as it is different now from a few years ago. Two generations of operating systems from now, the computer will have a strong visual input, recognizing not only the user, but also many other things in its field of view. People will communicate with the computer in the same way as they do with other human beings, that is, through words, body language and gestures. The computer will understand ordinary everyday English, French, German or any other major language. In such a world, there will no longer be any technophobes or computer illiterates – everyone will use a computer. There will be no need to teach specific computer skills.

However, computers do have a large part to play in education. Although they should not be an end in themselves, they can bring education to life. Virtual reality can be used to re-create historical situations, to take a class on a tour of the interesting places in the world or into space, or to wander around the inside of a molecule. Computers can illustrate ideas with moving graphics, gather and process information from global networks, and translate them into appropriate language for the ability of the individual child. They can put students in touch with teachers, regardless of the geographic location of either. They are the natural home of future artificial intelligence that will complement the teacher's talents, guide students through coursework, supplement the teacher's knowledge, and answer simple queries to liberate teachers to concentrate on individuals without the rest of the class sitting idle. Computers will enable students to explore information and to educate themselves, calling on teachers when they need extra help or special insight. Computers have infinite patience and time, and can easily adapt to the skill and knowledge level of individual children without making them feel backward. Children will not be afraid to ask questions of a computer they would not dare ask in front of a class of their peers.

Large screens will soon be cheap enough to be used extensively in education. A picture of the Taj Mahal may look impressive on paper or on a small computer screen, but blown up to several metres across on a video wall, with a friendly computer-generated guide to show the children around, it will have an enormous impact. Some schools may go the whole way and have rooms lined completely with screens to allow totally immersive environments to be re-created.

The network is the key to much of what computers can offer education. Without the network, computers can still use compact discs and on-board software to help students. But when they are connected to the network, they can access information from all over the world via the Internet. Further, they can connect children in one school to those in another, allowing non-geographic networks of children to be set up. Children from different countries can meet as if in the same room, which will doubtless be a valuable part of education itself, mixing cultures together and teaching the inter-national collaboration so important for many areas of life and work. Where particular teachers excel in a given area, they can share their special knowledge with children from all over the world, not just those that live nearby. Instead of a class of twenty, a lecture could be delivered via the Internet to tens of thousands simultaneously. Video capture of the lecture allows other children to see it later – it can stay part of the on-line knowledge base. Computers individually are useful, but when they are networked, that usefulness expands by several orders of magnitude.

Computers will help expand personal creativity, too. A child may have ideas of a tune long before they have the skills to write down the music or to play it on a piano. But with a computer filling the gaps in their skills, they can enter it into a computer just by humming. The computer can then help them explore its potential, improvising and mixing it, rearranging it and adding other instruments. We may possibly see many musicians emerge who would otherwise have been put off at the first hurdle by a lack of confidence. Similarly, in other fields, even in science and mathematics, computers would be able to carry out a great deal of research just by examining existing records, and could test out many hypotheses by modelling and number-crunching or by logic-checking. Creativity will not vanish when we have smart computers. It will be, rather, a deep source of personal enjoyment, as the computer helps us to achieve our full potential.

Work will change enormously in the next decade or two, as information technology, and other high technologies, make many existing jobs redundant. There is little point in training young people in the skills associated with, say, estate agents or travel agents since the Internet will make such occupations superfluous, as they are replaced by a small piece of software and a net connection. Many other skills will be similarly unnecessary. Occupations that are inherently human – caring professions especially – will take much longer to automate.

Unfortunately, not all children have access to computers now, and this will still be the case in the future. It will be many years before children everywhere have network access. Satellite communications will expedite progress, especially since some of the operators have already promised free access in developing countries. But equipment will still be scarce in many places, and so the inequalities of opportunity that exist now will unfortunately remain. All we can say with hope is that costs will continue to fall rapidly, and entry-level computers will become very cheap by Western standards, and will eventually be affordable a few years later in developing countries. With solar or clockwork power supplies, a lack of electrical infrastructure will not be a barrier, and, thanks to satellites, neither will the lack of wired networks. Once countries have joined the global information economy, their development may be swift.

Travel and Tourism

One of the most common predictions for the future is that travel will decrease and telecommunications usage will increase. The two are seen as opposite methods of achieving a common goal. Yet all the evidence is to the contrary. Letter-writing made it easier to conduct businesses from afar and thus increased travel and trade distances. Most businesses need to swap information between remote sites. Both improved letter services and the immediacy of the telephone enabled distant business operations to flourish. Industry only really broke free of its local roots and became national enterprises as these and other forms of communication improved. The use of the telephone made offices separated by hundreds of miles possible for a wide range of businesses.

However, road, air and sea transport were still needed to enable the human contact to be maintained. Thus, the telephone led to increased car use, not less. In a similar way, video-conferencing will make it easier to be in control of a international distant office. Because of this, air travel to deal with the social aspects of human interactions will be more frequent. We are still apes underneath with a need for social contact that remote presence does not satisfy. It will be a long time before communication replaces the experience of travelling or sharing a beer. Therefore, we expect to see a continuing and staggering rise in travel, air travel in particular.

One of the most frustrating part of travel today is the delay that seems inevitable at all stages. There is delay in buying tickets, delay in obtaining information, delay in contacting the office while on the move, delay in traffic queues and delay at the airport. These are precisely the things that a modern communications and computing environment can sweep away. The travel industry must be ready for the demand that will hit it.

Ticketless travel is far more than simply not having paper tickets. It is about being cocooned in an information environment from the moment you think of travelling to the moment you arrive at your destination. The problem for the travel industry will be to provide a service that makes the hassle of travelling disappear.

Some of the systems and technologies discussed in this book will have a major impact in the travel sector. To illustrate the point, imagine a journey in the near future (within ten years). When the traveller first starts to think about travel his or her intelligent computer agents will be out surfing the Internet to find the best package and to recommend routes and interesting places to visit. The agents could negotiate directly with suppliers, cutting out the margins for the middlemen. Security issues will be dealt with by recording an iris scan or fingerprint or, more radically, a chip under the skin. When the time comes to start the journey, the traveller's personal digital assistant will be informed by the airline when to start travelling to get through the traffic, and, *en route*, information on traffic congestion will be fed to an in-car system to ensure the journey is trouble-free. On arrival at the airport, security will be taken care of by remote scanning, obviating the need for tickets and passports. This will enable the traveller to proceed directly to the plane. There will be no need for buildings at the airport. People will not be waiting around to shop. Currently, they do so only because of the inefficient way they are handled. Unfortunately, this still leaves immigration and customs to deal with at the far end. However, the time spent on the plane or boat could be used to carry out remote checks, removing the need to queue and giving customs far more time to double-check the visitors. On arrival, the traveller's personal digital assistant will guide him to the pre-booked taxi (his agents have been at work again, behind the scenes, booking the taxi on the Internet), and will inform him of nearby restaurants and hotels that suit his budget and taste. At no point will this traveller feel out of touch with the world of information – that would be an adventure holiday indeed!

The advent of faster ferries, near-space air travel (planes that fly just above the atmosphere at far faster speeds than today) and the removal of time-consuming delays in the system will change the face of travel. Day trips to Australia from the UK will be possible, and a whole new dimension to travel will open up. It is the delay imposed by middlemen and poor IT systems that prevents easy travel and stops people from travelling as much as they would like. Tele-communications will increase the ability and desire to travel.

However, for the travel industry as it exists today there is a problem. Intelligent electronic agents that seek out deals on the Internet will replace many travel-related jobs. In fact, the industry has far more jobs that could be replaced by computers than any other sector.

What can people working in travel do to survive? Like many other information and service industries, they need to anticipate the switch from their traditional middleman role to that of being part of the 'caring' industries. Rather than being providers of tickets and brochures and holiday packages, they must become carers who ensure that you really do have personal attention, immediate backup and a smiling face wherever you go. They must ensure you are wrapped, not only in this information cocoon, but also in an environment that cares for your social needs. It will be a long time before the caring computer replaces these jobs, and they may be much more rewarding than handing out brochures or typing at terminals the way travel agents do currently.

Electronic Democracy

Northern Ireland has often been selected as a trial site for many technologies before wider deployment on the British mainland. It had the first all-digital network, and was the first region to replace all the cables between telephone exchanges with optical fibres. It was therefore a great disappointment to many of us working in IT that the 'Peace Referendum' of 1998 was conducted using paper voting slips. Electronic voting is a well-proven technology, and its introduction is long overdue, avoiding the long delays and frequent recounts of the current paper systems. Electronic voting is an important step in electronic democracy, but there is much more to democratic systems than just casting votes every few years.

In the UK, the 'Government Direct' initiative aims to bring a single point of call for administrative functions, linking all departments together for a streamlined operation, which is very commendable. Some long-term privacy issues await both recognition and official resolution, however. Once we have digital archiving of the records of every citizen, these will remain available, in principle, for ever. A future malicious administration would have access to integrated information on every citizen dating back many years, and in a form that was easy to use, allowing rapid identification of anyone considered a possible political threat.

But it is just this sort of information that is essential if we are ever to get true electronic democracy, and it is a price that we may have to pay, while trying to make appropriate safeguards. Abraham Lincoln defined democracy as government of the people by the people for the people. If he defined it today he might say the same thing. But in twenty years from now, such a definition might prove inadequate. By that time, we will share our world with conscious and artificially intelligent machines. The movement to protect the rights of at least the higher forms of animals, such as the apes, may well also have borne fruit by then. Those that we think of as part of the population might therefore be more than just people. A 2020 Abraham Lincoln might define democracy as government of the population for the population by the population. Certainly, it could well be the case that the best decisions were made by machines, and it may be possible to make sure that they have no bias. Power may corrupt people, but we do not yet know about machines. It may be possible to make a machine that could determine what everyone wants on an issue and take their views fairly into account when deciding what is best overall – maybe the greatest good for the greatest number, or whatever criteria we agree on.

Even using technology of today it would be possible to build a huge database that records the preferences of every individual in a society. We may start with a long tick list, but we could also select the defaults for a particular party, and then change those points where we may have a differing view. This preference list does not have to be just a simple tick list: it may allow us to choose and specify conditions, ifs and buts. We could state how strongly we care about something. In this way, we could build an electronic political shadow of ourselves. We could access and modify this at any time.

By inspecting the shadows, and checking any conditions, a government would then know what the population wants, effectively a referendum on every issue without the need for everyone to go out to vote. A machine could effectively represent the views of the population using this information. This capability has not yet been used, but there is no longer any good reason to hold back. If we truly want democracy, we need this sort of input. Otherwise we just elect a few representatives who can totally ignore our wishes for several years after we have counted the votes. Maybe eventually we could build a totally unbiased governor, a fly-by-wire democracy, but we will probably want to retain human controls for many years. Good government cannot always be about counting votes; it requires human judgment and wisdom. As yet, we have nowhere near enough understanding of how to make decisions for the greatest good. Complete automation of government may, therefore, be quite some time off. If our present governors realized this, they might stop treating such systems as a potential threat to their jobs, and might instead start reaping the enormous benefits that electronic democracy could bring to us all.

The Future of IT and the Developing World

With technology racing ahead, the wealth gap between the developed world and developing countries is increasing. More than half the world's population have yet to make their first phone call. However, there are strong grounds for optimism. A number of new technologies will enable much more rapid development than was previously possible. Some countries will move from developing to developed status in a relatively short time.

Historically, manufacturing industry has shifted around the world, capitalizing on lower wage rates in poorer countries that are sufficiently developed to cope with the basic manufacturing needs. These countries quickly develop skills and move up the wealth ladder. Until the recent economic crisis in Asia, there were strong signs that the region's technology would leapfrog that of the West, and it may yet happen.

India is often used to farm out information work. It is a huge call-centre for Western companies, taking bookings for British Airways, for instance; while Bombay is a centre for writing software for Western users. In spite of having only 1.3 telephones per 100 people, India is rapidly developing the key skills to thrive in the information economy. The global information economy offers hope to many other countries of similarly rapid development. A unique possibility is illustrated by the Tuvalu government, which sells its phone codes to companies offering expensive premium rate services. Now it has sold rights to its .tv web suffix. Together, the fees will bring in about £10,000 per inhabitant over the next few years. Unfortunately, such windfalls are rare and unlikely to be of much help to most countries.

Much of Africa has little or no industrial infrastructure. Many places have poor electricity, water, telecommunications and transportation systems, let alone high-tech factories. Building such an infrastructure would take a long time and would be expensive. And yet for a number of countries there is hope of jumping on to the global information economy very soon, rapidly becoming richer, and then investing in the basic needs of daily living. They could develop quickly by capitalizing on low-cost IT skills, not by retracing the steps of the Industrial Revolution.

The idea of someone in a remote village with no services working for a distant information company often invites ridicule, but it is perfectly feasible. Advanced IT skills can be learned quickly. Africa is rich in solar energy, and clockwork PCs are also now available. As for telecommunications access, even though some African countries have as little as one phone per thousand people, providers of low-earth-orbit satellite systems have already offered free access to their systems to residents in developing countries. So we can now imagine a scenario where a company in a developed country trains people in Chad as teleworkers, and provides them with a basic computer with free satellite-based telecommunications. These workers will have access to the Internet at up to 2Mbit/s, so they could do valuable web-site development, remote IT management, software production, information-processing or any other computer-based job. When they have enough money to buy their own equipment and have sufficient skills, they could publish their work worldwide on the same basis as anyone in any other country, or run global virtual companies. There is no need for them to emigrate to make money. To paraphrase the well-known cartoon: on the net, no one knows your head office is a mud hut.

There is another factor that favours the developing world in the information economy. The price of entertainment has rocketed compared with the cost of physical goods in recent years. And yet most video-based entertainment consists of reworkings of old ideas, or even repeats. It would be surprising if the vast, untapped cultural resources, stories and ideas in developing countries did not provide these nations with a high income in coming years. What they are lacking most is access technology, and it will be there soon, with someone else paying.

PART III

PROBLEMS, ISSUES AND THE FUTURE

The future is not going to be like the past, with just a few minor differences in colour or speed. It is going to be radically different. The future may not even have the one previous certainty – namely, us. As machines and people become intimately linked, first in the way society runs, and then later biologically, the future may be very different from our expectations.

Here we want to touch on some of the problems we are going to face that may need legal, moral or ethical decisions in the future. Some of them will challenge the essence of what we consider to be alive or human in the way we think about ourselves and others.

For a long time, science-fiction writers have played with many of the issues addressed in this section, but the progressive merging of man and machine will finally begin to happen in the twenty-first century. Because the law can take decades to react to major changes, many of the issues will be on us before we have recognized their full implications. It would be better if wider and more serious discussion started now, not after the first man-machine hybrids had struggled out of the realm of medical assistance into the wider world.

I

NEW PROBLEMS

Information Waves and Network Resonance

In many physical systems, a signal can feed back on itself and be amplified to create a resonant or runaway condition. The howl from a speaker when a live microphone is placed too close to it is a good example. Networks are no exception. Strange effects can often be seen in data networks as computers respond to signals that take a finite time to travel down the cables. The wrong combination of time spent in transit and time spent responding can, in the worst cases, lead to serious problems, even the complete failure of the network. Such problems have been observed in ATM queues and other places. Most of these effects are simply curiosities for the network engineer and are largely ignored by the majority of designers. After all, with the many different combinations of signal delay and response times or amplification mechanisms it is difficult to protect against everything. However, the emergence of automatic computer systems is beginning to create a whole range of problems that may force designers to look once again at the question of information waves.

The first class of potential problems arises from correlated traffic. A particular event or message may cause traffic to arise from a number of locations at or about the same time. The information wave is one manifestation of this. An announcement of a significant piece of information (such as a rise in interest rate) may trigger a financial-management software agent to make calls to banks, to buy or sell shares, etc. If just one agent makes such a call there is no problem. Even if a million humans were to make a call, there would still be no problem since networks are designed to withstand such traffic bursts from people, all of whom would dial at slightly different times. However, when a million computers, simultaneously running similar software at similar speeds, get the same information, they are likely to make the same decisions at the same time. The result may be a wave of call attempts spreading like a tsunami, at the speed of light. Some call-acceptance algorithms would be fooled into accepting a large proportion of these calls, bringing about a dangerous overload and a potential crash of the network. Of course, the network would soon be rebooted, but the computers would simultaneously detect this, and they would all make the same repeat attempt again, at the same time. The worst scenario would be that a message would have to be relayed over TV and radio asking people to switch their computers off and on, thereby re-introducing a degree of randomness. It is possible that a few blackouts in the United States may already have been caused by such an effect. While we have anticipated this particular problem, and can easily guard against it, there are an infinite number of ways in which such waves may result. It is an example of the sort of disruption that can arise when there is too much homogeneity in equipment or software.

Complex interactions between software may also cause traffic to grow spectacularly or in unexpected ways. Soon after software that could automatically relay messages to everyone on a mailing list became available, another piece of software allowed people who were going on holiday to set up an automatic response to messages that their computer received while they were away. A message arriving from a list server would then be replied to automatically, and the response would be relayed to everyone else on the list, bringing about another reply and another message, until either it was stopped by the list-server manager or the mailboxes filled up. We saw many cases of this effect, and many of us withdrew from mailing lists until a degree of discipline was introduced. Neither of the two pieces of software was faulty; there was just an unanticipated interaction between them. Again, there are an infinite number of potential interactions between software features, or data, and these cannot all be anticipated or prevented. As networks spread and computers become more versatile, such problems will inevitably increase.

Cyberwars and Cybernations

Some competing ideologies avoid violent conflict mainly by virtue of their geographical separation. However, in cyberspace, geographical boundaries are irrelevant, and people of different views are thrown together. Take, for example, Judeo-Christian and Islamic followers. Cyberspace conflict between the two groups has so far been avoided largely by the low penetration of Internet access, especially in Islamic areas. However, it is only a matter of time before conflict moves into this new domain, and we will then see various forms of information warfare. Some religions have many members, in many countries, and these will be among the first cybernations – nation-sized groups that are connected by networks and by common agreement rather than by geographical location. Many forms of tribalism could exist in cyberspace, and groups such as environmentalists or feminists could form cybernations, too.

The leadership of a cybernation would be able to communicate instantly with its entire membership, and of course it is also easier to expel people from a cybernation than it is to deport someone from a real country. This makes them potentially ideal states, where everyone is in touch, all working together, and everyone obeys the rules, powerful, yet highly defensible against attack. That is, except for cyberwars. These will be quite different from traditional wars. Geography will be irrelevant, and people on opposite sides may be living close to each other. Cyberwars, however, will differ in their lack of bloodshed. People, robots and agents will fight by attacking reputation and image, financial resources, control, access to information and any other information-related attributes, as well as computing, telecommunications and other electronic equipment belonging to the enemy; that is, just about everything the enemy has that involves information of any kind or a connection to the network. The biosphere would be left untouched. Of course, a cyberwar could escalate into physical conflict when real people are identifiable, or where a geographical location is considered more valuable to one side than the other, but it is quite possible for there to be no physical conflict whatsoever, with still a great deal of harm done.

II

New Issues

Computer-Generated Cyberspace

Cyberspace is a world inside the computer's memory; but it is designed mainly by humans, and so it reflects the ways in which people think about the world, and often reveals much about today's customs and procedures. Computers can construct and manipulate areas and objects in cyberspace, too, but they do so mostly under human guidance. A virtual building that has been designed by a human is not a computer creation, even if the computer has done the rendering, colouring, etc. It has still originated in a human mind. However, if a computer has designed a building automatically from general guidelines or from an evolved algorithm, then the final design is truly a creation of that computer.

Usually, this would not be of any great significance. A computer-generated design may not be all that different from human designs. It is only when the computer is able to explore freely that something radically new may come into existence. A machine that has evolved to fulfil a task without being restricted by human design rules could be very different, and could open up new areas of cyberspace. When this new creation is shown to a human, it might then extend or alter his ideas. The recent developments in evolution-based design may be seen as an important breakthrough in human knowledge, when the computer became a useful tool for creativity as well as for number-crunching. As we move further and further into the future, an increasing number of designs and inventions will be attributed to computers and eventually there will come a point where machine accomplishments exceed those of humans. Not long after that, it is likely that purely human contributions will be almost insignificant in our progress.

Computers and Sex (INTRO)

A key biological tool in evolution is sex. By mixing together genes from different parents, more combinations can be tried and an organism can adapt more readily to its environment. As with many ideas developed in nature, this has now been copied by computer programmers. By mixing together bits of parent programs, new programs can be constructed. Most of these will not achieve the goal, but just occasionally, a child program will accomplish the goal better than its parents. However, programmers are not constrained by nature. For instance, we asked why there are only two sexes in nature? Experiments with computers have shown that by using more than two sexes, or more than two parents, programs can be evolved faster than with one or two sexes. It all depends on the environment and the way the individuals can communicate and meet. In the computer, natural issues such as the energy expended on courting, the time spent finding a partner, loyalty, etc. all become irrelevant: computer programs can simply mate with the best. The net result is that evolution proceeds differently and faster with more than two sexes, three or four being optimal.

But it seems that information technology is affecting human sexuality, too. Advanced communications allow people to reach round the globe and meet (anonymously) with others of apparently similar feelings. Local, geographically based communities of support can be supplemented or even replaced by network communities. What previously might have been prevented by local cultural pressure can now be reinforced by the culture of a network community. People who once might have hidden their thoughts, feelings or behaviours are made increasingly aware that they are not alone, and can find others around the world who are similarly inclined. They may also learn of other behaviours that they did not even know existed, or they may become more inclined to experimentation. Whether such diverse sexual behaviours are genetic or cultural is largely irrelevant, since an environment in which different sexual expressions can be accepted is being created. One of our social predictions for the twenty-first century is that there will be a growing range of increasingly complex sexual preferences and behaviours.

Cybersex

A lot of people have experimented with verbal cybersex in discussion groups and shared spaces such as MUDs and MOOs. Many pretend to be the opposite sex while in these domains. Some do this for fun; some, to avoid harassment. Others try hard to prevent anyone finding out what gender they really are. Some take on different roles at different times, apparently without suffering any psychological problems. Artificial-intelligence entities, known as bots, also inhabit these areas, and many can make a reasonable pretence of being human, flirting with people quite effectively. Fortunately, most are still fairly easy to spot, and usually catch out only new users, but they will improve. Some people also pretend to be 'robots' so they can watch or interact with participants without arousing suspicion. So, we already see quite complex gender interactions, with heterosexual, homosexual, neutral, bisexual, asexual, the androgynous, the machine, the uncertain and the unknown all happily interacting with each other. Users can appear as they wish and can disguise their true identity or characteristics in many ways. With each of these pretending to be other than what they really are, or changing between genders dynamically, relationships in cyberspace can be very confusing indeed.

As technology permits more graphics, simpler man–machine interfaces and more artificial intelligence, we can expect the field to develop into terrifyingly complex relationships. On the Internet, no one knows you are a dog, or a robot, or whether you are six or sixty, fat or slim, ugly or attractive. A person's cyberspace avatar could have any desired appearance and behaviour. To further complicate things, around 2010–15 there will be external links to the human sensory system, with possibilities of new senses or new ways of stimulating existing senses in different ways. Still further, the body's mechanisms for sexual response are beginning to be understood, with the possibility of direct stimulation by manipulating nerve signals, chemically or electronically. The pleasure centre in the brain, the septal area, could be addressed directly, requiring no other stimulation to produce ecstasy.

If we combine these technological possibilities, not only is direct sexual contact unnecessary, but we can imagine that there would be no need for conventional sexual activity at all to produce a pleasurable sexual response. This implies great variety in future sexual rituals. Perhaps there may be some ridiculous relationships and sexual practices – imagine sending an orgasm by e-mail. Participants could be of any kind, human, machine or software, and there may be any number of 'genders' involved in a given sexual interaction, each with a given role. Flexibility is absolute in such a world.

The fact that sexual interaction across the network can be safe and novel, with few of the strings and conditions associated with real life, might make it very popular when technology catches up. But we can expect some real-life problems though. Already, marriages have been broken by cyberaffairs; and society does not yet have rules or conventions for network-based relationships. Just what is a healthy reaction of a woman who finds her husband has been chatting up a computer program for the last month?

Computers and Physics

One of the most common errors in predicting the future is to assume that we know all the physics that can be known, and that all that remains is effectively to fill in the gaps. It is salutary to study history and to find how many times this view has prevailed; but a moment's thought should make one realize how dangerous such an attitude is when entering the twenty-first century.

The physics we believe to be true is usually that which we can understand. It is shaped heavily by the brain's evolved tendency to see certain patterns and types of order in the world around us. It is limited by the form of the mathematics we use to analyse the world, and by our ability to understand what the mathematical symbols 'mean'. Our knowledge and the way our brains work limit the very experiments we can conceive to study the world.

Soon computers will be taking on an ever-larger role in analysing experimental data, collating results and even interpreting their meaning. As computer intelligence with human-like powers of reasoning develops there is absolutely no reason to assume that we will understand the physics figured out by the machines. They will discover new principles and rules that are beyond us. Probably, this will occur first in the study of chaotic systems or quantum mechanics, fields where even today many of the results are counter-intuitive. Supposed 'physical limits' today, such as the speed of light, may even be overcome.

It is entirely conceivable that physical phenomena will be exploited by computer-enhanced design, creativity and analysis that will completely change the future history of humankind; and while able to see the advantages, we will be unable to understand the mechanisms. It will present a major challenge to today's engineers and scientists who have been brought up with the rather arrogant assumption that everything is knowable and understandable.

Lamarckian Evolution

Before Darwinian evolution became the accepted explanation for biological change and adaptation, other models for how a system could learn and adapt existed. For instance, Lamarckian evolution – the inheritance of acquired characteristics – was one reasonable theory. The success of Darwinian evolution as an explanation of biology has led to the presumption that it is the only model, and this view has been propounded by some biologists. Quite clearly, however, silicon systems can be created that behave differently. Indeed, Lamarckian evolution could even be better for evolving computers!

Biological systems have rarely, if ever, evolved mechanisms that could allow information learnt from the environment to be mapped back into the genetic material. Presumably, the chemical mechanisms of memory and genetics are so different that evolution has not yet had time to discover how to combine the two. However, there is no reason to assume that this is neither possible nor desirable. When we design the equivalent of digital DNA it might be possible either to have functions that modify one's own DNA to take account of experiences, or to change the germ line DNA, or simply to store a cache of information that was passed on to the next generation to jump-start the learning process. In many ways, we could genetically reproduce the effect of cultural learning – which would effectively be a form of Lamarckian evolution with the store in the outside world.

The consequences of this would be profound. Computers that pass on their acquired behaviours genetically could evolve much faster than pure Darwinian evolution allows. The latter produces many genetic syntheses until a chance mutation appears in the right circumstances to survive better than its competitors. Studies of evolution as it could be, rather than as biology developed or limited it, may make the techniques applied to solving our problems that much more powerful. Lamarck was correctly shown to be wrong in explaining how biology works. That does not mean he could not be right in predicting how computer evolution could proceed.

Cybercreatures

Not all creatures need to have a physical presence. They may know nothing about the real world, and have no physical manifestation other than bits stored in memory somewhere, but would still be beings with a distinct existence. We may create pets, for instance, that live their lives exclusively in cyberspace; our agents may be thought of in this way. Some may interact with mental or physical space, via real-world interfaces, but others may not. Many such creatures have already been created. Artificial-life researchers worldwide have produced and evolved systems analogous to whole rainforests full of synthetic organisms with complex interactions. Genetic algorithms rely on creating new creatures or algorithms while killing off inferior offspring.

It is these evolved organisms, however trivial or insignificant they are today, that were the first cyberspace creations of our computers. They made up the first part of cyberspace that did not have to map on to a human being's mental space. Viruses were written by people and came out of their mental space, but these synthetic organisms evolved from their ancestors – humans did not design them. They were the first generation to be born in cyberspace.

These cybercreatures inhabit a part of cyberspace of which we have no concept, and no physical world equivalent. While they were evolved within a set of rules and constraints, we cannot imagine what they are like. They are just 'memory beings' – pure algorithm and data, no substance. Their lives may be (normally) short and under ultimate human control, but when they have strong artificial intelligence in the near future, and a degree of autonomy and initiative, they may need to be considered another life form. Soon we will have to make judgments of their rights. Should we be able to just switch them off? What other rights should they have?

Electronic pets, on the other hand, can be as much a part of our mental space as cyberspace. Programs may simply assemble some graphics on the screen for our benefit, but there would be no substance behind them. That is, the pet may have no deeper existence beyond these graphics. Others, however, may have this screen presence, but also a life in the background when they are not being shown on the screen. They may interact with other pets elsewhere; they may have agent properties; and they may even breed and evolve like other cybercreatures.

This highlights another aspect of cyberspace. Appearance is not necessarily fixed. A creature may be a pet for one person at one time, an agent at another time, and have no interaction with humans at others. It may have many simultaneous incarnations. Its visual appearance may change. The creature may have many different roles in just the same way as a person does. But since cyberspace is not limited by physics, these roles may be far more diverse.

III

WHAT IS HUMAN?

Our brain weighs approximately 1kg (2.2lb), is about 10cm (4 inches) in diameter and contains between 10^{10} and 10^{11} neurons. The only creatures with larger brains than humans are dolphins and whales; the largest carnivorous dinosaurs had brain cavities only a few centimetres in size; while the larger herbivores had remarkably small brains. Very little evolutionary analysis has been carried out on the human brain, despite the central importance placed on it as an explanation of the success of *Homo sapiens*. A number of deceptively simple questions have not yet been answered concerning potential limits to the effective size of the brain, or whether there are any underlying structural reasons why the brain is arranged in the manner it is.

Biological organisms function as information-processors; they take in information about the environment, process it, and then use that information to locate the necessary energy sources for survival. The more efficiently that organisms process and extract information from the environment, the more successfully they, and their off-spring, can continue their existence. These organisms are perpet-uated at the expense of less efficient entropy-engines. The last two billion years of information-processing have been driven by carbon-based molecular systems that have evolved through a combination of random mutation and selection, as described by Darwin. *Homo sapiens* has arisen through this molecular-based evolution. These observations lead to a further interesting possibility: if our brain is inherently limited by its carbon base, then the next step in 'evolution' might be to appropriate silicon as the intelligence medium. Further evolution would then be driven by mechanisms and forces radically different from those in nature.

The rapid development in silicon and biotechnology could soon bring the human race to a critical point in its evolution where it can break free of its biological roots. The potential impact is profound. The key thesis is that the remaining lifetime of both Darwinian evolution and *Homo sapiens* is short. We will, within the next fifty years, be able to seize control of our own evolution.

Homo sapiens has now reached a position where three significant developments could radically change the evolutionary mechanisms. First, as a species, it has learnt the fundamental concepts of evolution and thus can start using them, rather than be driven by them. Secondly, it has become able to manipulate its own genome directly, making Lamarckian evolution a possibility (although in this case the inheritance would be of desired, rather than acquired, characteristics). Finally, and most significantly, it has begun to create artificial-life systems that may eventually supplant the whole notion of carbon-based life. *Homo sapiens* is now able to take control of both the speciation process and the move from carbon to silicon life forms. We believe that this change is inevitable.

Most species are driven by the present evolutionary currents and the genome from which they have historically evolved. *Homo sapiens* is the first species to understand its own origins and, in doing so, is now able dimly to see its own future and to consider manipulating it directly by adjusting its own genome. Genetic engineering opens the possibility for a species that evolves through Lamarckian evolution – directly manipulating its offspring's genome to include traits the parents consider valuable. This gives us the potential to drive the evolutionary process where we choose, not by a slow and chance mutation driven by external pressure, but by a directive targeting.

Genetic engineering is viewed as a tool to gain robust, long-lived, disease-free, super-athletic bodies. We shall probably not see any profound change in our nature if this is the only use to which we put our evolutionary knowledge. But there are much deeper driving forces to evolution than simply lifespan, survival or health. The future evolution of *Homo sapiens* depends crucially on understanding the role that both energy- and entropy-processing play.

Homo sapiens has succeeded in occupying so many ecological niches because, among land animals, it has evolved the most powerful processor in relation to body size. Systems or organisms that are more efficient at information-processing could one day supplant Homo sapiens from this general environment. Notice that they do not need to have 'human intelligence' to process and use information about the environment more efficiently than Homo sapiens. A silicon chip, embodied in a suitable manner, may defeat a human through the sheer 'grunt' of massed information-processing without ever being labelled as 'intelligent'. This happens already in limited domains, such as chess-playing.

The key question then is can we improve our brains? The human genome project will be completed soon. At that point, a combination of human and computer search will be able to identify the genes needed to produce people of any chosen characteristics. Someone, somewhere will produce an élite race of smart, agile and disease-resistant people. We shall call this optimized human Homo optimus. While these people may not represent a new species in the strict sense, they may well think of themselves as such. They could be the first generation resulting from Lamarckian-style evolution, and thus would represent a key change of direction in evolutionary process. Unfortunately, the timing of their arrival could make them largely irrelevant, as we shall see.

Birth of a New Life Form: Silicon Systems

It is clear that the progress in silicon technology will continue for many years to come. If we simply extrapolate current trends, with progress continuing at current rates, we can expect the descendants of our desktop computers to be at least 50,000 times faster with at least 50,000 times more memory by 2015. By then, a typical machine will process information at about 5 million MIPS (million instructions per second) and have 1 TByte (Terabyte = 10^{15} bytes) of RAM. However, such extrapolation ignores the extra assistance that we can expect from computers as they progress. Ten years ago, computers began to assist with laying out circuits, and they now do this far faster than people. As they become faster and more capable, with access to a rapidly growing knowledge base and a growing range of tools, computers will assist and eventually replace us in more and more fields. Silicon devices will thus eventually drive the evolution of silicon, rather than carbon-based devices like us. So the figure of 50,000 may turn out to be a gross underestimate, and a figure nearer a millionfold increase over today's performance may be nearer the mark. In comparison, the limits referred to above give the human brain a processing power of around 1,000 million million operations per second, with a memory of 10 TBytes. We suppose that future computing devices will remain silicon based. This may not be true, and we acknowledge that other materials may prove better, and, indeed, there may be a move away from electronics to photonics, or a merging of the two, as well as links to carbon-based systems. The consequences, however, are largely material-independent since these alternatives are unlikely to replace silicon unless they improve processing speeds, storage density and power consumption per MIP, and speed up the rate of progress.

Computers are already helping us to become smarter. Without them we would have no understanding of fractals, chaos and other complex phenomena. But assistance from machines is not new – it has happened since we used the first tool. When all that we had were slide-rules or logarithm tables, the invention of the first computers was a big step that accelerated our calculations enormously. However, people were too short-sighted to see that eventually computers would become so fast and so cheap that they would revolutionize not only calculations in well-defined areas of arithmetic, but also all kinds of information-processing. Early electronics was almost entirely designed by man, but computers gradually took on board more and more of the design work, albeit mundane – checking logic here, routing a circuit there. They are still taking on more tasks, automating ever more of the work and freeing people from drudgery. In fact, we have now reached the point where our total reliance on technology is axiomatic. We seldom bake bread, smelt steel, weld cars or assemble TV sets by hand – machines do! Turn off the communications systems and computers and a large proportion of humankind would die!

Technology feedback will make succeeding generations of computers arrive faster, each successive generation helping even more in the development of the next. This is a feedback loop with a degree of feedforward – and it is positive. With the benefit of hindsight, we can see that it has applied throughout history. Many inventions or discoveries have not only been useful in their own right, but have accelerated progress within their fields (and often others, too). The more physics and mathematics we learnt, the more rapidly these fields developed. The more tools we made, the more tools we could make with them. The faster we could travel, the faster materials for making transport could be gathered. This continuing positive technology feedback in the computer-development cycle will accelerate development, with humans eventually cut out of the cycle completely. When a particular bottleneck prevents further develop-ment along a particular route (such as smaller device size), we will find other avenues to bypass the restriction, just as we always have done in the past.

This technology feedback will bring us super-smart computers very soon. Before they become as good as people at computer design, we can expect only slow acceleration in their evolution. However, being optimistic about human capabilities, we expect computers to surpass us in most fields by 2015. As we approach the point of human–computer equivalence, progress will accelerate faster. As we pass it, the progress curve takes a very rapid turn upwards, which will not cease until the development cycle is suddenly stopped by ultimate barriers imposed by physics – or by God. As yet, we are not aware of any such limits, so we expect computers at least millions of times smarter than us by 2030 – what they will achieve is guesswork.

We can expect these computers to change whole fields of communications, business and society. They will not, however, emulate human intelligence: rather they will develop in parallel, surpassing humans in many tasks for which they are best suited, opening new fields not currently accessible. We expect computers to evolve their own code and to rapidly move to a level of complexity beyond our understanding. Whether they are more intelligent than us will become as relevant as asking whether your car is as fast as your PC.

A mistake, which we often make in several fields, is to assume that progress will continue at today's rates. Consequently, we tend to put small advances in the near future and large advances in the very distant future – even centuries away. But technology feedback in computing will not only bring us smarter computers; it will accelerate development in *every* other field. Advances that might otherwise take many decades may require just a few months or years when we get ever-smarter computers. We should even ask ourselves whether it is worth tackling some big problems yet, since our lengthy efforts now may save only a very short time later. The only brake that is likely to occur is social breakdown or war, as was the case in the Dark Ages.

As growing computer intelligence accelerates progress in communications, materials, biotechnology, energy, robotics and cybernetics, earth and space exploration, developments in these areas will feed back positively into further computer development, which will impact back again into these fields. Positive feedback thus permeates the whole of technology. So we are about to enter an era of explosive technological development. Current research will yield earlier results. Technologies which were thought to be far in the future will be brought much closer. Scientific understanding will develop rapidly – though much of it may reside only within the computers and may be beyond our simple minds. How might this affect evolution?

In the same time frame in which we learn how to manipulate our own genome to produce *Homo optimus,* developments in computer technology will finally bring about smart machines. There are many possible routes to this realization and we cannot be certain which will win, but we can be sure that one of them will. We can expect the nature of this intelligence to have some similarities with our own, but not to be the same. Although intelligence in a machine does not equate with life as we know it, we may find that the differences are cosmetic, and we may begin to recognize intelligent machines as a new life form, another evolutionary offshoot of *Homo sapiens.*

As with all computers, and indeed all biological organisms, there will be a spread in levels of intelligence. Some machines will remain completely dumb; others may be much more sophisticated than ourselves. There will be many varieties of such machines, many species. The first generation or two will have been designed to assist humans. Their intelligence will be most useful, complementing our own, so that together we will advance into the future with greater speed.

The Future Evolution of Intelligent Life Forms
ROBOTUS PRIMUS

For a time at least, we will be the second smartest beings on Earth. Computers will probably surpass us in intelligence around 2015, and it will be some time after that before *they* develop the technology to bring *us* up to speed. So the first major impact will come from a new intelligence sharing the planet. We shall call this *Robotus primus.* In the 2015 time frame, it is reasonable to expect that these computers could be accompanied by a sufficiently developed robotics technology to make them fully mobile, though their 'minds' are not tied to any particular machine or location – but distributed. The early generations will rely on relatively crude robots, but these will quickly evolve into sophisticated androids. We stress that *Robotus primus* is not the robot itself, which is merely a tool, but the intelligent mind inside. We will of course see many grades of computer intelligence, just as we do now. A toaster cleverer than man would seem somewhat superfluous. The rapid formation of different types or 'species' of this artificial intelligence can be expected, with even élite models rapidly losing position to their descendants.

HOMO CYBERNETICUS

By 1995 scientists had already developed silicon chips which could interface directly with human nerve cells. Various cybernetic prostheses and other extensions to the body are in development.

Other scientists have demonstrated that thoughts can be detected and recognized, even without physical contact with the body. It seems reasonable to assume that it will not be long before a computer can interface directly with a human, producing artificial senses and possibly reading the person's thoughts. Although no one has yet demonstrated a means of putting thoughts into a human, it does not seem unreasonable to assume that it can be done, perhaps by creating appropriate electric fields at specific points, which again should not require any direct contact.

We thus expect that at some point after human–machine equivalence is achieved, the technology will be developed to make a full two-way mind-link between man and machine. Then we will be able to enhance our mental ability by using external processing as an adjunct to our own brains. Since by this time the machines will be far smarter than we are, this will represent a huge step for humankind.

Those people who accept this cybernetic technology will instantly have a great advantage over those who do not (and there will be many). In the same way that people rejecting IT today are a dying breed, future rejections may be more exaggerated and speedy. This is because as new technology arrives ever faster people will choose to use it or not more rapidly. Those who do not will be left behind at a much faster rate. The new species will be so far removed from *Homo sapiens* that it will in effect be a new breed, which we shall call *Homo cyberneticus*. As the technology rapidly develops, the differences between *Homo cyberneticus* and *Homo sapiens* will accelerate. However, since the early *Homo cyberneticus* is a conjunction of conventional humans with machines, there is obviously room for improvement.

HOMO HYBRIDUS

It is likely that many of the people who undertake cybernetic enhancement would lend themselves to genetic improvements, too, or would permit further development for their offspring. Another branch of optimized biological humans with some cybernetic links can therefore be expected. Perhaps their genes could be selected to work better with cybernetics than conventional organisms. We shall call this species *Homo hybridus*. This is the species that would make *Homo optimus* rather redundant, very soon after its creation. Similarly, the first generation of *Homo cyberneticus* would become obsolete, since the human bodies connected to the machines would be inferior to those of *Homo hybridus*.

Changes generally bring stress, and this often leads to conflict. The various new species would not coexist easily with those preferring to remain as *Homo sapiens*, who might even be renamed *Homo ludditus*, for obvious reasons. There would also be some competition for resources between these species. Whether peaceful coexistence is possible or not, it would seem unlikely, given the well-known nature of *Homo sapiens*. Science fiction has already begun to explore this conflict, with films such as *Terminator* and *Terminator 2* being famous examples. However, in *Terminator*, *Homo sapiens* wins, which seems an improbable outcome.

We can also expect friction within our species as machine intelligence improves. The Industrial Revolution reduced the value of muscle power, and in the same way, computer evolution will reduce the value of brainpower – to zero. One by one, jobs will be lost to machines, whether these be robots or computers. Our corporations will be run and staffed entirely by machines. Those using humans will not be able to compete and will go under. People will have fewer and fewer attributes to sell. Of course, production and output could greatly increase while human input could decrease, so we could all have a better quality of life without having to work. A fully automated economy could still be bigger than one that involves people. Twentieth-century economics will not work in the future – the cracks are already getting bigger; machines take out delay and uncertainty, displace humans, and reveal economics for what it is – a game of numbers in a spreadsheet. Our current concepts of wealth, money and ownership will all take a severe battering. Perhaps we will enter an age of leisure, where any work we do is voluntary and is based on spending time with other people. Or perhaps people will be overtaken by fear as they lose control over what is happening. Then revolts might break out. In any case, this age will not last for long because we will be absorbed into the higher existence offered by the machine world.

When a direct link from the computer into the human brain is achieved, thought-transmission could give us telepathic communication not only with machines but also with other people. We may be able to enjoy a shared consciousness with other humans and synthetic intelligences such as *Robotus primus*. Our evolution will therefore be set against the background of a global consciousness. Individuals will still exist, but we will also share a group existence. As we achieve this link, we will also be able to make copies of our minds in the machine world – a backup in case of accident. We will become immortal, even if our mobility and physical existence is restricted until a suitable replacement body or android is produced for us. Death will be just a memory of a primitive past.

We may have one alter ego stored in the machine, or we may have many. We may try out different situations or life decisions, or different personalities. These alter egos could occasionally make trips into the 'real world', time-sharing robotic bodies. These bodies would not necessarily be humanoid, so we could really be the 'fly on the wall'. Procreation could be a highly creative act, with any number of people combining selected characteristics from themselves or their imaginations to generate new beings. Each person could give rise to large numbers of personal offspring in this way. The number of beings which could coexist may be limited by the size of the host infrastructure, but they could time-share or lie dormant until more space is created.

HOMO MACHINUS

The two enhancements of biological optimization and connection to synthetic intelligence are not equal in their potential impact. Due to speed of development, we can reasonably assume that some of each of the above species would exist, but we can also argue that they would soon become obsolete. *Homo optimus* would have been left behind by *Homo cyberneticus*, and this species in turn would be succeeded by *Homo hybridus*. However, as the mind–machine link became completely transparent, and as materials and cybernetic technology improved, *Homo hybridus* would rapidly find most of its intelligence and physical capability residing in the machine half rather than in the organic half. As the human mind gradually moved further into the machine world, it would become apparent that the organic body was redundant. If it died, it would be a minor inconvenience, requiring a cybernetic replacement to be commissioned. As the organic body died out, *Homo hybridus* would, too, become a non-corporeal being, which we shall call *Homo machinus*.

This new species could retain some elements of the earlier human race, but it would be vastly more intelligent and would have access to whatever physical capability it required. It could travel at the speed of light, exist in many places at once, and would be essentially immortal. It would coexist with *Robotus primus*, but we could expect that the two species would interact and eventually converge.

Human Evolution: The Future

Summarizing, we can draw an outline of, or a projection of, human evolution from the distant past to the relatively near future. Space exploration is currently prohibitively expensive, so we have not got far yet. However, when we exist only as information within a machine, we could be copied into a minute device, and then encapsulated in a very small shell with some nano-technology machines – nanites. By this time, we could expect that nanites would be able to make replicas of themselves, and of anything else we desire. These small shells would be like seeds. We could accelerate them to near light speeds and send them off to other planets circling distant stars. The nanites would be able to fabricate a suitable environment and body for us, and then upload us into them. The environmental requirements of *Homo machinus* might not be very demanding. We might not even be limited by the speed of light, if we could master warp drive, wormholes or tachyon transmission, all of which have been postulated by physicists and are known to be possible in principle. Surely a few years of research by mid-twenty-first-century super-beings will crack the problems of turning these principles into functional devices. Many other exciting areas previously beyond us will be a natural part of our everyday existence.

It is certain that there will be strong reaction to this tinkering with the human species. Not everyone will welcome it, either for religious or ethical reasons, or through simple preference. Many people will dissociate themselves from genetic manipulation or cybernetic technology. These people will remain as conventional *Homo sapiens*. They would at best have to coexist with these other human offshoots, who would dwarf them mentally and physically. They would not be able to compete, and they could have the same relationship to the human variants as pets do with us today. Knowing that they, too, could at any time accept the new technology and move on to the higher planes of existence would probably rapidly diminish the numbers of *Homo sapiens*. The race might just fizzle out due to lack of interest after a couple of centuries of stubborn resistance, say by 2200. *Homo sapiens* would be the first species on Earth to have become voluntarily extinct.

There are limits to *Homo sapiens*, and limits to the environmental stress our planet can withstand, and as a species we may be close to extinction, to be replaced by a whole range of silicon life forms. As computers become more powerful they will take over, first driving their own technological developments through automated design and self-evolving programs, and then in other fields. Once free of carbon, or aided directly by silicon, the whole pace and nature of evolution will change.

Currently, there are arguments that machines (in their present form) can never equal man's intelligence. These arguments are about as relevant as those of previous centuries relating to the number of angels that can sit on a pin head, or indeed more recently, to the existence and nature of hell. If machines beat us at processing information, and all the indications are that they will increasingly do so, they may never need to directly equal our intelligence – they need only to circumvent it. They may also work out how to be 'similar' to our brains for themselves through the sheer processing power they possess. Early estimations of when this might happen made widely inaccurate assessments of human brainpower. This should not obscure the inevitability of the process. One hundred years is very short in evolutionary terms.

A combination of technology feedback and human limitations will soon change the fundamentals of society and biology. *Homo sapiens* does not cope well with predicting or understanding exponential changes; many will fail to see the future coming until it is the past.

Today we enjoy a rich environment of male and female, ethnic variety, cultural and educational backgrounds – a real society of minds! Soon this richness, limited by a given cerebral volume and the way different functions reside in each of the two lobes of the brain, will be augmented by a third lobe – the machine. Thinking in a new way, and possessing new abilities, we will see our potential and imagination lifted. The question is: can we overcome our mental stasis through a symbiosis with machines, or will we go down fighting and be wiped out?

Glossary

AI Artificial intelligence, or machine intelligence – the ability to accomplish things on a machine that we would otherwise consider to require intelligence. Some humans redefine intelligence to be those things that a computer cannot do. The goal is not generally to produce synthetic human intelligence, but to accomplish the same functions by synthetic means. Ideally, machines would have complementary skills so we could work as a partnership, but increasingly it looks like there will eventually be little left that we can do that machines cannot.

API Application programming interface – a set of instructions available to a programmer from the supporting platform. In our case, the networking instructions made available to allow programmers to drive network functions.

Asimov's laws of robotics Science-fiction writer Isaac Asimov (1920–92) proposed that robots should be constructed so that they follow some basic rules:

o   A robot may not injure humanity or, through inaction, allow humanity to come to harm.

1   A robot may not injure a human being, or through inaction, allow a human being to come to harm, except where that would conflict with the Zeroth Law.

2   A robot must obey the orders given to it by a human being, except where that would conflict with the Zeroth or First Law.

3   A robot must protect its own existence, except where that would conflict with the Zeroth, First or Second Law.

Since then, various extensions to these basic laws have been proposed. The important thing is that we should be very careful when building smart machines.

ATM Asynchronous transfer mode. When data is transmitted between machines, there are a variety of techniques available. Some protocols allow the machines to transmit continuously until all the data has been sent, but most modern techniques break up data into packets. ATM and TCP-IP both do so. The packets have a header section containing an address and a small amount of other information, followed by the payload section holding the data being transmitted. Along the way, equipment such as routers can read the packet headers and direct them along the right route. ATM uses short packets, usually called 'cells', with a fixed length of 53 bytes (a byte is 8 bits, that is, ones or zeros, the header.

Darwin, Charles (1809–82) Botanist who theorized about evolution through natural selection. In a competitive environment, those organisms that had variations that made them better adapted would be more likely to live long enough to reproduce so these variations would be inherited by the next generation. For instance, giraffes with slightly longer necks would be able to reach leaves that shorter giraffes could not, and would be more likely to survive times of food shortages.

DECT Digital European Cordless Telephone – a cordless telephone standard, used mainly for short distance connections between a handset and a node connected to a fixed line. The handset works within a zone a few hundred metres (1,000 ft) in diameter. Some phones have both DECT and GSM capability and can switch automatically to the GSM when they are out of range of their local node.

DNA Deoxyribonucleic acid. DNA is the self-replicating material located in the nucleus of every cell in all organic living things (at least on Earth), and it holds the genetic information that describes how to make them. It has also been used as a chemical computer, and shows some potential as an information-storage medium, too.

EPAC Electronically programmable analogue circuit – a type of reconfigurable circuit that uses analogue components instead of digital ones.

FPGA Field programmable gate array – a type of reconfigurable digital chip. The chips do not have a preprogrammed function, but can be programmed in the field for whatever function is required, subject to the number of gates available.

GSM Group Special Mobile or Group Switched Mobile, according to taste – a digital cellphone standard, used in many countries, including most of Europe.

Lamarck, Jean-Baptiste de (1744–1829) Botanist and zoologist who proposed that animals pass on the characteristics they have acquired during their lives to their offspring, including changes of body structure caused by use or disuse of parts. For instance, a giraffe that regularly stretches its neck to reach the highest branches would have offspring with longer necks.

LAN Local area network – localized network that links various computers and associated equipment together. There is no rigid size limit to LANs, but typically they are restricted to just a few buildings.

...ype of display that uses long molecules that
...ı an electric field is applied, changing the way they

which 5 bytes are

...ıange trading systems – a local-community economic system.
...ı slightly more professional form of a babysitting circle where people
...ge tokens for each other's work and earn tokens by doing work for others.
...ey are proliferating rapidly. Although they do not use national currencies, tax
authorities are showing increasing interest in the value of the transactions.

MIPS Million instructions per second – a very crude measure of a digital chip's performance. In modern computers, many factors contribute to performance, so this measure is rarely used.

MOO Object-oriented MUD.

MUD Multi-user domain, formerly multi-user dungeon – an area of cyberspace where people can meet and interact. Originally, they were mostly used for games of dungeons and dragons.

NC Network computer – a computer that relies on the network for much of its functionality. Files and programs can be stored on a server and accessed by the NC when needed. The idea is to have a single point of software and file maintenance, centralized control, and lower specification of terminal, with lower overall costs. Some designs are basically a PC without a hard disk drive.

Net-PC Effectively, an NC that does not have stripped-down functionality – a realization that stripping down does not actually save much, so why not keep the power? Instead, the PC is optimized for network use.

Passive picocell This is a device that converts a light signal from an optical fibre to a radio signal, and that can also modulate the light signal with the returning radio signal. It is passive because no power supply is required. It allows small zones with very high capacity to be created.

PC Personal computer. Most PCs are based on the IBM standard set in the early 1980s, though there are many alternatives with smaller market shares.

PDA Personal digital assistant. This is a very portable computer designed for use on the move for making notes, directories and diaries, as well as an increasing number of other applications. Some higher-specification PDAs now include cell-phone technology to allow mobile access to the Internet, electronic mail etc.

RAM Random access memory – the main form of memory in most computers.

Star architecture A type of wiring where each node has a separate wire that runs all the way back to the switch.

T1000 An android on the film *Terminator 2* made up of a fluid metal. The fluid could reform into any shape and take on any appearance. It could in principle be made using Robodyne Systems' fractal robot technology. (In the film, the creator of the robot was Cyberdyne.)

TByte Terabyte – one million million bytes.

TCP-IP transmission control protocol–internet protocol. IP is another packet-based protocol (*see* ATM) for exchanging data between machines. The packets are longer than ATM cells and have longer headers. The packets can be of variable length, but typically they hold about 1 Kbyte of data. Internet protocol specifies the structure and coding of the packets, especially the headers, so that they can be handled correctly by the many different machines that have to deal with the packets. For instance, it makes sure that all machines use the same structure for addresses and so on. The TCP bit is concerned with the overall progress of the transmission. It makes sure that when the packets arrive, they are sorted into the right order and that none are missing or corrupted. If there is a problem, it ensures that packets are retransmitted. So, TCP-IP together makes sure that data is put correctly into packets, finds its way to the destination, and is checked and reassembled into a meaningful transmission at the other end.

TV Television – a primitive video-based entertainment system. Although it has been purely a broadcast medium until recently, with no user interaction, new forms that use digital encoding allow a degree of interactivity.

VR Virtual reality. This is a three-dimensional computer-generated environment, in which the user may be given a feeling of immersion, and can wander around as if inside the computer.

WDM Wavelength division multiplexing. This is the use of different wavelengths (or colours) of light on the same fibre at the same time, rather like different frequencies of radio share the air. Using a number of wavelengths can increase fibre capacity without having to increase the speed of electronic components at the ends.

Further Reading

Anderla, G., Dunning, A. and Forge, S., *Chaotics*, Adamantine Studies of the 21st Century, 1997

Blumenfeld, Y., *Towards the Millennium: Optimistic Visions for Change*, Thames & Hudson, 1998

Cochrane, P., *108 Tips for Time Travellers*, Orion Business Paperbacks, 1997

Didsbury, H. F. (ed.), *Future Vision: Ideas, Insights, and Strategies*, World Future Society, 1996

Martin, J., *Cybercorp: The New Business Revolution*, Amacom, 1996

May, G. H., *The Future is Ours*, Adamantine Press/Praeger, 1996

McLaren, J., *Press Send*, Touchstone, 1997

Mercer, D., *Marketing Strategy: The Challenge of the External Environment*, Sage, 1998

————, *Future Revolutions*, Orion, 1998

Naisbitt, J. and Aburdene, P., *Megatrends 2000*, Sidgwick & Jackson Ltd, 1990

Petersen, J. L., *Out of the Blue*, The Arlington Institute, 1997

Index